LETTICE
&
LOVAGE

Other plays by Peter Shaffer

FIVE FINGER EXERCISE
THE PRIVATE EAR AND THE PUBLIC EYE
THE ROYAL HUNT OF THE SUN
BLACK COMEDY
THE WHITE LIARS
SHRIVINGS
EQUUS
AMADEUS
YONADAB
WHOM DO I HAVE THE HONOUR OF ADDRESSING?
(Radio)

LETTICE & LOVAGE

A COMEDY BY
PETER SHAFFER

A Cornelia & Michael Bessie Book

HARPER & ROW, PUBLISHERS, New York
Grand Rapids, Philadelphia, St. Louis, San Francisco
London, Singapore, Sydney, Tokyo, Toronto

FIRST U.S. EDITION

Designed by Alma Orenstein

LIBRARY OF CONGRESS CATALOGING-IN-PUBLICATION DATA

Shaffer, Peter, 1926–
    Lettice and lovage: a comedy / Peter Shaffer.
      p. cm.
    ISBN 0-06-039098-0
    ISBN 0-06-096342-5 (pbk.)
    I. Title.
PR6037.H23L4   1989   88-45724
822'.914—dc20

90 91 92 93 94 CC/MPC 10 9 8 7 6 5 4 3 2 1
90 91 92 93 94 CC/MPC 10 9 8 7 6 5 4 3 2 1 (pbk.)

To Leo,
who asked for a comedy,
and
for Maggie,
who incarnates comedy
with love

INTRODUCTION

Lettice & Lovage is the first comic play I have written since my farce set in the dark, *Black Comedy*, composed in 1964 and incidentally also containing a part written for Maggie Smith. It is obviously a very English piece, and I have not therefore tried too hard to Americanize it. The task would be wrong-headed. I can only hope that audiences here will enjoy it with half the glee they evinced in London; that they will embrace Lettice and find Lotte sympathetic.

This latter exercise may be more difficult. New York (and other cities in the United States) is lucky to possess an immeasurably better contemporary architecture than exists in England, and the controversy across the ocean may appear to Americans to be excessive. They may be assured that it is not. The buildings erected in my country since the war have been, almost without exception, shameful—a shoddy disgrace to the land which produced Messrs. Wren, Hawksmoor, Vanbrugh, and Nash, not to mention the legion of anonymous builders who created the glory of countless English villages. In America I have seen several structures which celebrate the artistic eyes and hands of the late twentieth century: I have not seen one such in England. Since *Lettice & Lovage* first appeared in 1987, the concern and rage of Lotte Schoen has become something of a general passion with English people—partly, or perhaps largely, because of the same concern and rage so ringingly expressed by the Prince of Wales. In this regard therefore the play proved to be surprisingly and particularly ahead of its time. It has been very pleasurable for its author to watch it acquire a certain prophetic aura!

This version contains a significant rewrite. In the original, played for a year with huge success by Maggie Smith and Margaret Tyzack at the Globe Theatre, London, the two ladies were left at the end preparing to blow up a select list of modern architectural monstrosities with a petard—a medieval explosive device. This fantastic conclusion produced much laughter, but I was always aware of how assiduously it had been tacked onto the play in order to do just that. It was a forced climax, dismissing the piece into improbability. Over the ensuing months I came to disapprove of it for this reason, and spent much time considering more natural endings. Finally the present one was born, and seemed to me both correct and pleasing. It is also, in our lunatic world, entirely credible. I look to see a variant of E.N.D. Tours Ltd. advertised in the *New York Times* any day now!

With this rewrite Lettice prospers, and Lotte prospers with her, and their progenitor is happy. I wish them a long and mirthful life among new friends.

In conclusion, I would like to thank most deeply my director Michael Blakemore—a master vintner who understands how to press enchanting wine from the grapes provided.

PETER SHAFFER

CHARACTERS

LETTICE DOUFFET

LOTTE SCHOEN

MISS FRAMER

MR. BARDOLPH

A SURLY MAN

VISITORS TO FUSTIAN HOUSE

The action of the play takes place in the Grand
Hall of Fustian House, Wiltshire, England; Miss
Schoen's office at the Preservation Trust, Architrave Place, London; and Miss Douffet's basement flat, Earl's Court, London.

First performed at the Theatre Royal, Bath, on October 6, 1987, and subsequently at the Globe Theatre, London, England, under the management of Robert Fox Ltd, the Shubert Organization, and Roger Berlind, with the following cast,

LETTICE DOUFFET	Maggie Smith
LOTTE SCHOEN	Margaret Tyzack
MISS FRAMER	Joanna Doubleday
MR. BARDOLPH	Richard Pearson
A SURLY MAN	Bruce Bennett
VISITORS TO FUSTIAN HOUSE	Alex Allenby, Joanna Doubleday, Jennifer Lautrec, Barbara Lewis, Maxine McFarland, Lindsay Rodwell, Shelagh Stuttle, Nick Sampson

DIRECTOR	Michael Blakemore
DESIGN	Alan Tagg
COSTUMES	Susan Yelland
LIGHTING	Robert Bryan

ACT ONE

SCENE 1: A

[*Elizabethan music sounds; lugubrious and mournful.*

The curtain rises on the Grand Hall of Fustian House: a gloomy sixteenth-century hall hung with indistinct portraits of the Fustian family, and dim copies of a coat of arms above them.

The main feature is an imposing Tudor staircase of oak. A scarlet rope is stretched across the bottom, denying access to the public.

To the left—as the viewer sees it—is a stone archway; to the right another archway leads to the way out. It is a damp, freezing gray day and the house is unheated. As the music groans with melancholy, a small group of miserable tourists is led in from the left by their guide, Miss LETTICE DOUFFET. *She is a lady in middle life, appointed by the Preservation*

1

*Trust to show people around this dreary place. She
wears clothes of a slight theatricality and boldness,
in contrast to her hearers, who are encased in rain-
coats and plastic hats and carry umbrellas. At this
moment her natural exuberance has been somewhat
conquered by the house and weather, but she is still
striving to deliver herself dutifully of the text which
she is employed to recite and which she has memo-
rized.*]

LETTICE: [*Moving to the staircase and rubbing her arms
against the cold*] We come now to the most remarkable
feature of Fustian House. This is the Grand Staircase,
constructed in 1560 out of Tudor oak. It consists of
fifteen stairs, made from planks, cut at the neighboring
sawmill of Hackton. The banister displays an ogival pattern, typical of the period. The plaster ceiling above is
embellished with a design of love-knots, also typical.

[*All look up without interest. A man yawns. A
woman stares at her watch.*]

Please note the escutcheons, placed at intervals around
the cornice. These bear the family motto in Latin:
Lapsu surgo, meaning, "By a fall I rise." This alludes to
an incident which occurred on the Feast of Candlemas
1585 upon this actual staircase. On that night Queen
Elizabeth the First, making a Royal Progress through
her realm, chose to honor with her presence the yeoman merchant John Fustian. To mark the occasion Fustian caused a banquet to be laid here in this hall, and
himself stood by the Queen's side at the top of the stairs
to escort her down to it. However, as Her Majesty set

foot on the first stair she tripped on the hem of her elaborate dress, and would have fallen, had not her host taken hold of her arm and saved her. The Queen being in merry mood immediately called for a sword and dubbed him a knight of her Realm.

[*The man yawns again, loudly. Others also yawn.*]

This concludes the tour of Fustian House. On behalf of the Preservation Trust I wish you a good afternoon.

THE PUBLIC: [*Drowsily*] Good afternoon . . .

[*They file past her dispiritedly.* LETTICE *looks after them in dejection. The light fades and the lugubrious music returns. The crowd of tourists walks around the stage, shedding outer garments, reversing them or putting on new ones.*]

S C E N E   1 :   B

[*Lights up again. It is some days later; a little brighter weather.* LETTICE *stands just as before, with a new group of listeners—the same people with different hats, scarves, and glasses—but equally bored. Among them is a young husband and wife; the wife carries a baby in a sling.* LETTICE *herself is bored, and recites her text in a mechanical monotone, much faster than before.*]

LETTICE: We come now to the most remarkable feature of Fustian House. This is the Grand Staircase, constructed in 1560 out of Tudor oak. It consists of fifteen stairs, made from planks cut at the neighboring sawmill of Hackton. The banister displays an ogival pattern typical of the period. The plaster ceiling above is embellished with a design of love-knots, also typical.

[*All look up as before, without interest. A man scratches himself. A woman coughs.* LETTICE *presses on desperately.*]

Please note the escutcheons placed at intervals around the cornice. These bear the family motto in Latin: *Lapsu surgo,* meaning, "By a fall I rise." This alludes to an incident which occurred on the Feast of Candlemas 1585—

[*The baby suddenly starts crying. The mother tries to hush it. All the tourists crowd around it in concern.* LETTICE *is ignored.*]

[*With sudden ardor, making up her mind*] Please! You are looking in fact at a unique monument of English History! Yes, indeed. And one of the most romantic . . . It is known as the *Staircase of Advancement!* . . . Does anyone know why it is so called?

[*They stare at her in silence. One or two shake their heads and murmur, "No."*]

I will tell you. On that day of Candlemas—which by the way has nothing to do with Christmas, as some of you may think, but falls on the second day of February— John Fustian gave a great feast in this hall to honor Queen Elizabeth. We do not know what he served at this banquet, but no doubt it contained hedgehogs.

[*The scratching man is startled. A woman cries out in disgust.*]

THE MAN: Hah?

LETTICE: Certainly. Hedgehogs were a considerable delicacy in those days. They were known as "urchins" and would have been endored. Do you know what that word means—"endored"?

[*The crowd murmurs, "No."*]

Made golden! Glazed with egg yolk. An exquisite word, do you not think? . . . They were imaginative, our ancestors, in what they ate. Their food is a particular enthusiasm of mine. [*To a woman*] Do you know they also ate puffins?

THE WOMAN: Good heavens!

LETTICE: They classified them as fish so they could eat them on Fast Days of the Church. Clever, you see. The same with coney—similarly classified. You know what coneys are?

THE WOMAN: I'm afraid I don't . . . Pine cones, perhaps?

LETTICE: No, no, no—much juicier! [*Conspiratorially*] Infant rabbit, taken from its mother's womb.

THE WOMAN: Oh, no!

LETTICE: The Romans called them *lauraces,* and they were reputedly delicious.

THE WOMAN: How disgusting!

LETTICE: We are in no position to find other ages disgusting, I fancy. I resume my story . . . Her Majesty arrived for John Fustian's feast, emerging from the bedchamber at the head of the stairs. She was wearing a dazzling dress with a hem onto which had been sewn one hundred pearls, dredged from the Indian Ocean, and sent as a present by an Ottomite sultan! Alas, so heavy was this hem that she tripped on the first step and would have fallen the whole way down, had not her host, who was standing in the middle of the staircase—on the seventh stair from the top, can you see it?—

[*All peer upward and murmur "Yes!" They are now interested.*]

had he not rushed up and caught her in the very nick of time. For this service the Queen immediately called for a sword and dubbed him Her Knight! She then tore off the six largest pearls from her treacherous hem and bade him set them in the handle of the sword which had just ennobled him. [*Pause.*] You would have seen that sword in the next room, couched on a bed of crimson velvet, but unfortunately it was stolen last week. An interesting story, is it not?

HER HEARERS: [*Agreeing, pleased*] Oh yes! . . . Yes, indeed . . . Charming . . .

LETTICE: Thank you very much.

HER HEARERS: Thank *you!*

LETTICE: This concludes the tour of Fustian House. On behalf of the Preservation Trust, I wish you a good afternoon.

HER HEARERS: [*Gratefully*] Good afternoon!

[*She smiles at them happily. The lights fade as sprightlier Elizabethan music springs up. The tourists now march cheerfully around to it, again changing their clothes.* LETTICE *takes off an outer garment to greet warmer weather.*]

SCENE 1: C

[Lights up again. Music fades. It is again some days later, brighter yet. LETTICE, *as before, is lecturing another group of the public but this time it is clearly a pleased and larger audience. Her own manner is also now confident and happily dramatic. Only one man in the group, standing a little apart—a surly-looking creature in a cap and raincoat—is growing increasingly suspicious and restive as her recital goes on.]*

LETTICE: You are looking now at what is indisputably the most famous staircase in England! . . . The *Staircase of Ennoblement!* On the night of February the second, 1585—a brilliant snowy night—John Fustian laid before his sovereign here in this hall a monumental feast! The tables were piled high with hedgehogs, puffins, and coneys!—and a hundred of the liveliest courtiers stood salivating to consume it! *[Increasingly excited by her tale]* Suddenly she appeared—Gloriana herself, the Virgin Queen of England!—encrusted from bosom to ankle with a blaze of diamonds presented to her by the Czar Ivan the Terrible, who had seen a portrait of her in miniature and lost a little of his icy heart to her chaste looks! Smiling, she set foot upon the first stair, up there! Alas, as she did so—at that precise moment—she slipped and would have plunged headlong down all fifteen polished and bruising steps, had not her host—standing precisely where I stand now, *at the very bottom—leapt in a single bound* the whole height of the staircase to where she stood and saved her!

[*One or two gasp with amazement.*]

Imagine the scene! Time as if suspended! A hundred beribboned guests frozen like Renaissance statues, arms outstretched in powerless gesture! Eyes wide with terror in the flare of torches! . . . And then suddenly John Fustian moves! He who up to that moment has lived his whole life as a dull and turgid yeoman, breaks the spell! Springs forward—upward—rises like a bird—like feathered Mercury—*soars* in one astounding leap the whole height of these stairs, and at the last possible moment catches her in his loyal arms, raises her high above his head, and rose-cheeked with triumph cries up to her: "Adored Majesty! Adored and *En*dored Majesty! Fear not! You are safe!—And your hedgehogs await!"

[*This recital produces a reaction of pure joy in her hearers, some of whom actually applaud. The* SURLY MAN, *however, is not impressed. He speaks in a whine of hostility.*]

SURLY MAN: Excuse me.

LETTICE: Yes?

SURLY MAN: Could you give me your reference for that story?

LETTICE: My what?

SURLY MAN: Reference. I'm by the way of being an Elizabethan scholar. The doings of the Virgin Queen constitute my hobby. I have nowhere read that John Fustian leapt up that staircase, let alone lifted her on high or spoke those words.

LETTICE: It is true nevertheless.

SURLY MAN: I don't see how it can be.

LETTICE: What do you say?

SURLY MAN: For one thing, no one in the world could leap those stairs in a single bound. An Olympic athlete couldn't do it.

LETTICE: Excuse me, but there is a hostility in your voice which implies that what I am saying is an untruth. That it is lacking in veracity.

SURLY MAN: It's lacking in possibility, that's what it's lacking in. I ask you again for your reference, please.

LETTICE: [*a little flustered*] Well . . . the Chronicle, of course. The Fustian Family Chronicle!

SURLY MAN: And where may I find that?

LETTICE: You mayn't.

SURLY MAN: Why not?

LETTICE: Because it is not published. It lies hidden in a private Archive. Safe from the eyes of those who would use it for aggressive and uncharitable purposes.

[*The others murmur with approval. Sounds of "Hear! Hear!" "That's right," etc. They look at the* SURLY MAN *with dislike.*]

This tour is now at an end. Please take that way out. As you go you will observe a saucer on the maplewood table by the door. It is from the very first period of the Wedgwood factory: hence its delicate shape and shade. Its purpose is for the collection of such [*elaborate accent*] *pourboires* as you may care to leave. If, as is possible, some of you lack the French tongue, I translate that word as—

SURLY MAN: Tips.

LETTICE: [*Sweetly*] Tokens of appreciation.

[*She smiles sweetly at him. He marches off crossly.
The others thank* LETTICE *effusively, shaking her
hand or warmly saying good-bye as the lights fade.*

*Lively music. The crowd again mills around the
stage deftly changing into summer attire.* LETTICE
puts on a colorful scarf.]

SCENE 1: D

[*Lights up: a brilliant day, with yet more Tourists.*
LETTICE *is again lecturing—now entirely in control—and her public listens enthralled! To one side,
holding a guidebook, stands* LOTTE SCHOEN: *a se-
vere-looking lady in her late forties, her dark hair
and dress both aggressively plain.*]

LETTICE: The incident I have just described to you—in
which the Virgin Queen Elizabeth was saved from almost certain death by a feat of daring completely una-
chievable today *by even the greatest Olympic athlete*—
is only one of many deeds of high drama which have
been enacted upon the stage of this historic staircase.
[*Pause.*] Not all of them, alas, were so happy in their
outcome. The ensuing century was in every way
darker, and the doings on its staircases were corre-
spondingly more murky . . . It was upon these very stairs
one hundred years later, that the most *terrible* of all

events connected with this house occurred—on Mid-summer morning, sixteen hundred and eighty-nine.

[*All look expectant.* LETTICE *warms to her tale.*]

This day was intended to celebrate the marriage of Miss Arabella Fustian to the handsomest young lordling in the region. The bride was a radiantly beautiful girl of eighteen—"the catch of the County," as she was called. On the morning of her wedding her father, Sir Nicholas, stood exactly where I stand now—waiting to escort his only daughter to the church. The door of the bed-chamber opened above

[*She points; all look eagerly.*]

and out stepped this exquisite creature in a miasma of white samite. It is not hard to imagine her father staring up at her, tears welling in his old eyes—she about to descend these stairs for the last time a maiden! And then—ah, suddenly! a terrible drumming is heard! A frantic pounding along the oak gallery—and toward her, galloping at full speed, is Charger, the faithful wolf-hound of the family, wild with excitement at smelling the nuptial baked meats roasting in the kitchen below! In his hurtling frenzy he knocks the girl aside! She stag-gers—flails the air—shoots out her hand for the banis-ter, which alas is too far from her, and *falls headlong* after the beast! . . . her lovely body rolling like a cloud down the fifteen stairs you see, until at last with one appalling jolt it comes to rest at her father's feet! . . . [*She points to the spot, at her own.*] No Mercury he, but ancient and arthritic, he stoops to touch her. Is she

dead? No, the Saints be praised! Her neck is unbroken.
[*A pause.*] In a dreadful echo of the gesture with which
his ancestor won the family title, he catches the girl up
in his arms and, watched by the agonized dog, carries
her upward to her room. A room she was never to leave
again. Arabella regained consciousness, yes, but her
legs, which had danced the Gavotte and the Scotch Jig
as no legs had ever danced them, were now twisted
beneath her in mockery of the love-knots which grace
the plaster ceiling above you!

   [*All look up.*]

By her own choice the girl immured herself in that
chamber up there for life, receiving no visitors but
howling incessantly the Marriage Hymn which had
been specially composed for her by Henry Purcell himself! . . . The Family Chronicle records that her atten-
dants were all likewise distorted. I quote it for you.
"The wretched lady would employ as domestics only
those who were deformed in the legs and haunches:
knotted women, bunchbacks, swivel-hips, and such as
had warpage and osseous misalignment of the limbs."
Servants of all shapes clawed their way daily up this
staircase, which was now known no longer as the Staircase of Aggrandizement, but the *Staircase of Wound
and Woe!* This name it has retained ever since.

   [*A pause.* LOTTE *finally speaks, unable to restrain
   herself any longer.*]

LOTTE: This is intolerable.
LETTICE: I beg your pardon.
LOTTE: I find this absolutely intolerable!

LETTICE: I'm sorry? I don't understand.

LOTTE: Miss Douffet, is it not?

LETTICE: That is my name, yes.

LOTTE: Yes! Well, I would like to speak to you at once, please—in private.

LETTICE: On what subject?

LOTTE: I said private, please.

LETTICE: I find this extremely odd. I am not used to having my tours interrupted with brusque demands.

LOTTE: [*To the public*] Would you please excuse us now? It is most urgent that I speak to this lady alone. The tour is at an end at this point anyway, I believe.

LETTICE: It is. But its conclusion is a graceful adieu, not an abrupt dismissal. And it is spoken by me.

LOTTE: I'm sorry but I really have to insist. [*To the public*] Please forgive me, but I do have the most imperative business with this lady.

[*She looks at them hard, and her look is very intimidating.*]

Please.

[*They stir uneasily.*]

LETTICE: [*To the public*] Well—it seems I have to let you go—regrettably without ceremony. What can be so urgent as to preclude manners I cannot imagine! I do hope you have all enjoyed yourselves.

[*Murmurs of enthusiastic assent: "Oh yes!"* . . . *"Thank you!"* . . .]

The way out is over there. You will find placed by the exit a Staffordshire soup-bowl into which, if you care to, you may deposit such tokens of appreciation as you feel inclined to give. Thank you and good-bye.

THE PUBLIC: Good-bye, Miss . . . Good-bye . . . Thank you . . .

[*They go out, bewildered and extremely curious, looking back at the two ladies. As the last one disappears,* LOTTE's *manner becomes even colder.*]

LOTTE: You are not permitted to receive tips, I believe.

LETTICE: I do not regard them as that.

LOTTE: What then?

LETTICE: What I called them. Some people are appreciative in this world. They warm to the thrilling and romantic aspects of our great History.

LOTTE: Others, however, warm to accuracy, Miss Douffet. And others again—a few—are empowered to see that they receive it.

LETTICE: I don't understand you.

LOTTE: Myself, for example. My name is Miss Schoen, and I work for the Preservation Trust. In the personnel department.

[*A pause.*]

LETTICE: Oh.

LOTTE: Reports have been coming in steadily for some time now of bizarre inaccuracies in your tour here. Gross departures from fact and truth. I have myself today heard with my own ears a generous sample of what you have been giving the public, and every one of those reports falls far short of what you are actually doing. I can hardly think of one statement you made in my presence that is correct.

LETTICE: The gastronomic references for a start. They are all correct. I would like you to know I am an expert in Elizabethan cuisine.

LOTTE: [*Crisply*] I am not talking about the gastronomic references—which in any case form no part of your official recital. Today I listened to a farrago of rubbish unparalleled, I should say, by anything ever delivered by one of our employees. The whole story of John Fustian's leap upstairs, for example, concluding with his actually feeding fried hedgehogs into Queen Elizabeth's mouth directly from his fingers. As for the tale of Arabella Fustian—that is virtually fabrication from beginning to end. The girl was crippled by a fall, certainly, but it is not known how she fell. Her engagement was broken off but it is not known why, or who broke it. And so far from staying in her room singing thereafter, she lived to become a respected figure in the vicinity, noted for her work among the poor. The composer Henry Purcell was not, to my knowledge, involved in her life in any way.

[*A pause.*]

Well? . . . What do you have to say?

[*A longer pause.*]

LETTICE: I'm sorry—but I cannot myself get beyond your own behavior.

LOTTE: Mine?

LETTICE: What you have just done.

LOTTE: I don't understand.

LETTICE: What you have done here, Miss Schoen, today.

I don't mean your rudeness in interrupting my talk, unpleasant as that was. I mean coming here at all in the way you have. Pretending to join my group as a simple member of the public. I find that quite despicable.

LOTTE: I beg your pardon?

LETTICE: Deceitful and despicable. It is the behavior, actually, of a spy.

LOTTE: Well, that is what I am. I came here with that specific intention. To observe unnoticed what you were doing.

LETTICE: To spy.

LOTTE: To do my duty.

LETTICE: Duty?!

LOTTE: Precisely. My duty . . . The precise and appropriate word.

LETTICE: To embarrass your employees—that is your duty? To creep about the Kingdom with a look of false interest, guidebook in hand—and then pounce on them before the people in their charge? Is that how you conceive your duty—to humiliate subordinates?

LOTTE: This is a sidetrack.

LETTICE: It is not. It really is not!

LOTTE: A total sidetrack and you know it! *My* behavior is not the issue here. Yours—*yours* is what we are discussing! It is that which needs explaining! You will report tomorrow afternoon at my office in London. I believe you know the address. Fourteen, Architrave Place. Three o'clock, if you please.

LETTICE: [*Alarmed*] Report? . . . For what? Report? . . . I don't understand. What do you mean?

[*Pause.*]

LOTTE: [*Coldly*] I suggest you now attend to the next group of tourists awaiting you. And that you confine yourself strictly to the information provided by the Trust. I will see you at three tomorrow. Good afternoon.

[*She goes out.* LETTICE *stands, appalled.*]

LETTICE: [*Calling after her, in rising panic*] I . . . I'm to be tried, then? . . . I'm to be judged? . . . Haled to Judgment?

[*A pause.* MISS SCHOEN *has gone.*]

[*In dismay*] Oh, dear.

[*A grim music. Lights fade.*]

SCENE 2

[*Miss Schoen's office at the Preservation Trust in London. The following afternoon. At the back is a central door. On the walls are framed posters of some of the great houses owned by the Trust. At her desk sits* MISS SCHOEN *looking darkly through a pile of letters: an official file lies before her. Three o'clock sounds from Big Ben outside.*

There is a faint knocking on the door.]

LOTTE: [*Sharply*] Yes?

[*The faint noise continues.*]

Yes?! Is there anyone there?

[*The knock sounds a little louder.*]

Yes. Come *in!*

[*The door opens timidly.* MISS FRAMER *enters: a nervous, anxious assistant, frightened, breathy, and refined.*]

FRAMER: [*A whisper*] It's me, Miss Schoen.

LOTTE: What?

FRAMER: [*Just louder*] It's me, Miss Schoen.

LOTTE: Miss Framer, I do wish you could learn to knock audibly. Not scratch at the door, or fumble at it like some kind of rodent.

FRAMER: I'm sorry, Miss Schoen.

[LOTTE *raps sharply on the desk, three times.*]

LOTTE: That is a knock! Do you understand?

FRAMER: Yes, Miss Schoen.

LOTTE: Then copy it. Alert me to the fact that you wish to enter.

FRAMER: Yes, Miss Schoen.

LOTTE: Now what is it?

FRAMER: [*A whisper*] Miss Douffet is here to see you.

LOTTE: What?

FRAMER: [*Louder*] Miss Douffet is here to see you.

LOTTE: Ah.

FRAMER: I asked her to wait.

LOTTE: That was enterprising of you.

FRAMER: Thank you . . .

LOTTE: How does she seem to be?

FRAMER: Bold, I would say.

LOTTE: Bold?

FRAMER: Her clothes are bold . . . Well, bolder than mine anyway.

LOTTE: I see . . . Did you have a talk with Mr. Green about her, as I asked you to?

FRAMER: Oh, yes, indeed.

LOTTE: He did the original hiring, I understand.

FRAMER: Yes, that's right.

LOTTE: [*Brisk*] Well? And?

FRAMER: He says when he met her for the first time this spring he thought she might make a valuable addition to our staff of guides. She appeared to be mad on history.

LOTTE: Just mad would seem to be more like it, judging from these letters.

FRAMER: Oh, dear . . .

LOTTE: Does he know nothing about her at all?

FRAMER: Nothing whatever, it seems.

LOTTE: Well, this file is worse than useless. It just gives her address and nothing else. [*Consulting it*] Nineteen Rastridge Road, Earl's Court . . . Do you know it?

FRAMER: I'm afraid not.

LOTTE: A singularly dreary street. What I would term Victorian Varicose.

FRAMER: [*Laughing sycophantically*] Oh, that's good! That's very good, Miss Schoen. Victorian Varicose! Oh, yes, indeed. Most amusing!

LOTTE: [*Ignoring the flattery*] But if she's a Londoner, what is she doing working in Wiltshire?

FRAMER: I think it was the only position available. Apparently Fustian House isn't particularly popular with our guides. It was just for the summer.

LOTTE: I see . . . [*Suddenly touching her head*] Oh, God.

FRAMER: [*Fussing*] What? What is it?

LOTTE: Nothing.

FRAMER: Is it one of your headaches?

LOTTE: [*Brisk*] No.

FRAMER: Is there anything at all I can do?

LOTTE: No, thank you.

FRAMER: Perhaps an aspirin. Shall I get you an aspirin, Miss Schoen?

LOTTE: Nothing, thank you. Stop fussing! If you want to help, bring me a cup of tea. Strong.

FRAMER: Of course!

LOTTE: And one for that woman out there. She's going to need it.

FRAMER: Yes, Miss Schoen.

LOTTE: Show her in, please.

FRAMER: Yes . . . Yes . . . At once . . . I'm sorry.

[MISS FRAMER *goes out.* LOTTE *shakes some cologne from a little bottle onto a handkerchief and applies it to her temples. After a moment three loud knocks are heard and* MISS FRAMER *shows in* LETTICE DOUF- FET. *She is wearing a black beret and a theatrical black cloak like some medieval abbot. She carries a leather satchel and is very uneasy.*]

LOTTE: Ah, Miss Douffet, good afternoon. Please sit down.

[LETTICE *sits in a chair facing* LOTTE.]

I hope you had a pleasant journey up to London.

LETTICE: That is not very likely, is it?—considering one is about to be arraigned.

LOTTE: I'm sorry?

LETTICE: I'm at the Bar of Judgment, am I not?

LOTTE: Your position is to be reviewed, actually. I'm sure you see the inevitability of that. I have no choice in the matter.

LETTICE: Like the headsman.

LOTTE: I'm sorry?

LETTICE: The headsman always asked forgiveness of those he was about to decapitate.

LOTTE: I would really appreciate it if we could exclude historical analogies from this conversation.

LETTICE: As you please.

LOTTE: It is, after all, solely to do with your job and your fitness to perform it. We both know what we have to talk about. As an official of the department which employs you I cannot possibly overlook what I witnessed yesterday afternoon. I cannot understand it, and I cannot possibly condone it. Do you have anything to say in extenuation?

[*A pause.*]

LETTICE: It is not my fault.

LOTTE: I'm sorry?

LETTICE: Except in a most limited sense of that word.

LOTTE: Then whose is it?

LETTICE: I respect accuracy in recounting history when it is moving and startling. Then I would not dream of altering a single detail.

LOTTE: That is gracious of you.

LETTICE: In some cases, however, I do confess I feel the need to take a hand . . . I discovered this need working at Fustian House this summer. It is wholly the fault of that house that I yielded to it.

LOTTE: Of the house?

LETTICE: Yes.

LOTTE: You are actually blaming the house for those grotesque narrations?

LETTICE: I am. Most definitely. Fustian House is quite simply the *dullest house in England!* If it has any rival in that category I have yet to discover it ... It is actually *impossible* to make interesting! Not only is its architecture in the very gloomiest style of Tudor building, *nothing whatever happened in it!—over four hundred years!* A queen almost fell downstairs—but didn't! A girl did fall—not even downstairs—and survived to be honored by the poor. How am I expected to make anything out of that?

LOTTE: You are not expected to make things *out* of the house, Miss Douffet. Merely to show people *around* it.

LETTICE: I'm afraid I can't agree. I am there to enlighten them. That first of all.

LOTTE: Enlighten?

LETTICE: Light them up! "Enlarge! Enliven! Enlighten!" That was my mother's watchword. She called them the three Es. She was a great teacher, my mother.

LOTTE: Really? At what institution?

LETTICE: The oldest and best. The Theatre.

[MISS SCHOEN *bristles.*]

All good actors are instructors, as I'm sure you realize.

LOTTE: [*Cold*] I'm afraid I don't at all.

LETTICE: But certainly! "Their subject is Us—Their sources are Themselves!"—Again, my mother's phrase. She ran a touring company of players, all trained by her to speak Shakespeare thrillingly in the French tongue.

LOTTE: The French?

LETTICE: Yes. She moved to France after the war, unable to find employment in her native England equal to her talent. We lived in an agricultural town in the Dordogne. It was not really very appreciative of Shakespeare.

LOTTE: The French peasantry is hardly noted for that kind of enthusiasm, I understand.

LETTICE: Nor the intellectuals either. Voltaire called Shakespeare *barbare*, did you know that? Barbarian.

LOTTE: I'm not surprised. The Gallic mind imagines it invented civilization.

LETTICE: My mother set out to correct that impression. Her company was called, in pure defiance, "Les Barbares"!

LOTTE: She was evidently not afraid of challenge.

LETTICE: Never! Every girl was trained to phrase faultlessly.

LOTTE: And every man also, one presumes.

LETTICE: There were no men.

LOTTE: You mean it was an all-girl company?

LETTICE: Indeed. My mother married a Free French soldier in London called Douffet, who abandoned her within three months of the wedding. She had no pleasure thereafter in associating with Frenchmen. "They are all fickle," she used to say. "Fickle and furtive."

LOTTE: A fair description of the whole nation, I would say.

LETTICE: She brought me up entirely by herself. Mainly on the road. We played all over the Dordogne—in farmhouses and barns, wherever they would have us. We performed only the history plays of Shakespeare, because history was my mother's passion. I was the stage manager, responsible for costumes, props, and sword fights. Fights, I may say, as ferocious as they can only be, enacted by a horde of Gallic girls in armor when their dander is really up! She herself was famous for her King Richard the Third. She used to wear a pillow on her back as a hump. It was brilliantly effective. [*Springing up*] No one who heard it will ever forget the climax of her performance—the cry of total despair wrung from her on the battlefield! [*Stooping, to imitate the royal hunchback*] *"Un cheval! Un cheval! Mon royaume pour un cheval!"*

[LOTTE *stares astounded.*]

All the translations were her own.

LOTTE: A remarkable achievement.

LETTICE: Not for her. Language was her other passion. As I grew up I was never permitted to read anything but the grandest prose. "Language alone frees one," she used to say. "And History gives one place." She was adamant I should not lose my English heritage, either of words or deeds. Every night she enacted for me a story from our country's past, fleshing it out with her own marvelous virtuosity! . . . Richard's battlefield of Bosworth, with the golden crown hung up in a thornbush! King Charles the First marching to his beheading like a ramrod on a freezing January morning, wearing two shirts of snowy white linen, lest if he trembled from cold his enemies would say it was from fear! . . . [*Rapt*] Wonderful! . . . On a child's mind the most tremendous events were engraved as with a diamond on a windowpane! . . . And to me, my tourists—simply random holidaymakers in my care for twenty minutes of their lives—are *my* children in this respect. It is my duty to enlarge them. Enlarge—enliven—enlighten them.

LOTTE: With fantasies?

LETTICE: Fantasy floods in where fact leaves a vacuum.

LOTTE: Another saying of your mother's?

LETTICE: My own! . . . When I first went to Fustian House I spoke nothing *but* fact! Exactly what was set down for me—in all its glittering excitement. By the time I'd finished, my whole group would have turned gray with indifference. I myself turned gray every afternoon! . . . Fustian is a Haunted House, Miss Schoen. Haunted by the Spirit of Nullity! Of Nothing Ever Happening! . . . It had to be fought.

LOTTE: With untruth.

LETTICE: With anything!

LOTTE: [*Implacably*] With untruth.

LETTICE: [*Grandly*] I am the daughter of Alice Evans Douffet—dedicated to lighting up the world, not dousing it in dust! My tongue simply could not go on speaking that stuff! . . . No doubt it was excessive. I was carried—I can't deny it—further and further from the shore of fact down the slipstream of fiction. But blame the house—not the spirit which defied it!

LOTTE: And this is your defense?

LETTICE: Where people once left yawning they now leave *admiring.* I use that word in its strict old sense—meaning a State of Wonder. That is no mean defense.

LOTTE: It is completely irrelevant!

LETTICE: Last month I put out a soup-bowl by the rear exit. Not from greed—though heaven knows I could be forgiven that, with what you pay me. I wanted *proof!*

People express gratitude the same way all over the world: with their *money*. [*Proudly*] *My soup-bowl brims!* It brims every evening with their coins, as they themselves are brimming! I watch them walking away afterwards to the car park, and those are *Brimming People*. Every one!

LOTTE: [*Tartly*] Really? If you were to look through these letters you might discover quite a few who were not actually brimming—except with indignation.

[LETTICE *approaches the desk and examines a letter.*]

LETTICE: Churls are always with us. Curmudgeons are never slow to come forward.

LOTTE: [*Furious*] *Twenty-two letters!* I have twenty-two letters about you, Miss Douffet! . . . None of them exactly written in a state of wonder!

LETTICE: [*Loftily*] Twenty-two—what's *that?* . . . I have fifty—sixty! Here—look for yourself! Here! . . . Behold! . . . Here!

[*She grabs her satchel and empties its contents over the desk—a small avalanche of envelopes.*]

Vox populi! The Voice of the People! . . . I wrote my address beside my soup-bowl. This is the result!

LOTTE: [*Protesting*] Please, Miss Douffet! . . . This is my desk!

LETTICE: [*Hotly*] Read them. Read for yourself! . . . *There* is my defense. The Voice of the People! . . . Read!

LOTTE: [*Exploding*] *I will not! I will not!* This is nonsense—all of it! They don't matter! . . . None of this matters—your mother—your childhood—your car park—*I don't care!* [*Pause; struggling to control her-*

self] I am not in the entertainment business—and nor are you. That is all. We are guarding a heritage. Not running a theater. That is all.

[*She glares at* LETTICE. *Three violent knocks are heard on the door.*]

Yes! . . . What?

[MISS FRAMER *comes in nervously, bearing a tray of tea with scones, butter, and jam.*]

FRAMER: The tea, Miss Schoen.

LOTTE: [*Calmer*] Would you like some tea?

LETTICE: That would be kind.

LOTTE: As strong as you can make it for *me,* please, Miss Framer.

FRAMER: Yes, Miss Schoen.

LETTICE: [*Brightly to* FRAMER] So strong you can trot a mouse on it, my mother used to say.

FRAMER: Oh, that's good! That's very good! "Trot a mouse"! . . . Oh! Did you hear that, Miss Schoen?

[*She and* LETTICE *laugh conspiratorially together until* LOTTE *gives her an icy look.*]

LOTTE: Miss Framer, please.

[*The laughter dies.* LOTTE *picks up one of* LETTICE's *envelopes. She reads the enclosed letter.*]

FRAMER: [*To* LETTICE] There's a scone and jam, if you would like.

LETTICE: Have you no marmalade?

FRAMER: I'm afraid not.

LETTICE: You really should, in this office. It's a much more historical preserve. Do you not know the origin of that word?

FRAMER: Marmalade? I'm afraid not.

LETTICE: *You* know it, I'm sure, Miss Schoen.

LOTTE: What?

LETTICE: The origin of the word "marmalade."

LOTTE: Regretfully, no.

[*She returns to reading the letter.*]

LETTICE: [*To* FRAMER, *undeterred*] Mary Queen of Scots. She was frequently sick with headaches—

[FRAMER *glances at* LOTTE.]

—as who could blame her, poor confined woman? Each time she fell ill she would call for a special conserve of oranges and sugar. Her maids would whisper among themselves in French, "Bring the preserve—Marie is sick! *Marie est malade!*" . . . Do you see? *Marie est malade*—marmalade!

FRAMER: Oh, yes! Too extraordinary! . . . You should perhaps take some when you have one of your headaches, Miss Schoen.

LOTTE: Thank you, Miss Framer; that will be all for the present.

FRAMER: Yes, Miss Schoen.

[*She hurries from the room.*]

LETTICE: [*Drinking her tea*] Do you have headaches?

LOTTE: [*Reading*] Now and then, yes.

LETTICE: I'm sorry.

LOTTE: We all have something.

LETTICE: Your assistant could be right. Perhaps what eased Queen Mary could also help you.

LOTTE: Perhaps.

LETTICE: Which letter is that? The one that says I light up the corridors of the past as with a blazing torch?

LOTTE: No, this is the lady in the green sweater.

LETTICE: [*Dashed*] Ah yes . . .

LOTTE: [*Reading aloud*] "Dear Miss, I was the lady in the green sweater last Wednesday afternoon to whom you explained the portrait of a boy wearing leaves in his hair. It was so fascinating to learn the truth about that picture. If I had not asked I would never have learned that terrible story of the young heir murdered by his uncle with a garland of poisonous herbs. I had never realized that one could actually kill people through the scalp in that way. How clever it was of you to remind me of the extraordinary death in *Hamlet* where the old King is poisoned through his *ears*. It just goes to show that Shakespeare thought of everything first . . ."

[*A pause.* LETTICE *looks at her and smiles self-excusingly.*]

LETTICE: The Trust itself admits that boy's end was mysterious.

LOTTE: You must see yourself—it's no good, any of this. As I said, we are not running a theatre. If you were a playwright you could legitimately stand by your soup bowl and expect to see it filled for your invention. To some people—incomprehensible as it is to me—that is not only allowable but even praiseworthy. A tour guide however is not a paid fantasist, and in her such an action remains merely dishonest.

LETTICE: I cannot accept "merely" . . . I do not do anything *merely!*

LOTTE: Untruth is untruth. It will find no endorsement in
this office. Now let us not go on with this.

LETTICE: Read one more letter. The one in the blue en-
velope. The writer is a director of the Royal Shakespeare Company. He says adventure is in the air whenever I open my mouth.

LOTTE: That is entirely the trouble.

LETTICE: Why trouble?

LOTTE: Please! This is unpleasant enough.

LETTICE: Yes! Of course! I understand! We live in a country now that *wants* only the *Mere.* Mere Guides. Mere
People. Mere Events. I understand completely!

LOTTE: Miss Douffet, let me be frank. [*Pause.*] There is no
possible way I can justify your continued employment
with the Trust.

[*A long pause.*]

LETTICE: So. I am condemned.

LOTTE: You are found, regrettably, unsuitable.

LETTICE: When do I leave?

LOTTE: Right away, I think, would be best.

LETTICE: I could finish the summer. There's not so very
much of it left.

LOTTE: On balance I would rather you didn't.

LETTICE: I see. Well. Good. Yes. Of course . . . It is really
the more merciful way, I grant you that. Instant obliv-
ion.

LOTTE: Please now, Miss Douffet!

LETTICE: No, no, you are kind in your ruthless way. You
don't leave one, as some tyrants might do, to languish

in the prison of false hope. Away with her to sudden and peremptory death! . . . I thank you!

LOTTE: [*Exasperated*] Oh, for God's sake! Can't we dispense with theatrics for just one moment? You are, after all, only going to another job.

LETTICE: [*Suddenly crying out*] *Really?* . . . Am I? . . . And where do you imagine I shall find that—at my age?

[*A long pause.*]

LOTTE: I will try to compose a reference of some sort for you.

LETTICE: Please do not. I would not ask you to lie on my behalf.

LOTTE: I wouldn't lie, Miss Douffet. Something no doubt can be thought up.

LETTICE: That is not your forte, Miss Schoen—thinking things up. At the moment you exude a certain gray integrity. Please do not try to contaminate it with color.

LOTTE: [*Through gritted teeth*] You are not fair. You are not fair at all. Not at all!

LETTICE: [*Rising*] I have joined the ranks of the Unemployed. Fairness is not one of our salient characteristics.

[LOTTE *presses the buzzer. It is audible.*]

I leave you with a true story concerning color. Check it in the books, if you like, for accuracy. Are you aware how the Queen of Scots behaved at the moment of her execution?

LOTTE: Without theatrics, I hope.

LETTICE: Not at all. Quite the reverse. It was the custom for victims on the scaffold to shed their outer garments to avoid soiling them with blood.

[MISS FRAMER *comes in.* LETTICE *includes her in the story.*]

Queen Mary appeared in a dress of deepest black. But when her ladies removed this from her—what do you imagine was revealed?

LOTTE: I really can't guess.

LETTICE: [*To* MISS FRAMER] Can you?

[*The secretary shakes her head helplessly: No!* LETTICE *begins to loosen her cloak.*]

A full-length shift was seen. A garment the color of the whoring of which she had been accused! The color of martyrdom—and defiance! *Blood red!*

[*She steps out of her cloak to reveal a brilliant red ankle-length nightdress, embossed all over with little golden crowns.* MISS FRAMER *gasps.*]

Yes—all gasped with the shock of it! All watched with unwilling admiration—that good old word again—all watched with *wonder* as that frail captive, crippled from her long confinement, stepped out of the darkness of her nineteen years' humiliation and walked into eternity—a totally self-justified woman! [*To* LOTTE] That is strict and absolute fact. A long good-bye to you!

[*She sweeps up her cloak from the floor and walks triumphantly out of the office.* LOTTE SCHOEN *stares after her in amazed fascination.* MISS FRAMER *stands astounded. The curtain falls.*]

END OF ACT I

ACT TWO

[Lettice Douffet's basement flat in Earl's Court, London. Several weeks later.

Entry to this flat, as with many Victorian houses in London, is achievable only through the front door of the house on street level above, and thence down a staircase. We can see this staircase, dingy and covered with linoleum, whenever LETTICE *opens the door to her flat. Also clearly visible is a large bay window through which can be seen a typically drab "area"; a section of the pavement above it, with street lamp; the steps going up to the front door on one side of it; and the legs—just the legs—of anyone walking past the house or entering it. Indeed, a man walks by as the curtain rises, establishing this.*

The room is poorly furnished, but contains several curious theatrical relics, including a sword and two thrones—one in plain wood, one gilded. On the wall is a flamboyant poster advertising, "La Compagnie Etonnante LES BARBARES *Dans le Drame le Plus Hor-*

rifique de Shakespeare: RICHARD III. *Avec la Grande Vedette Anglaise* ALICE EVANS DOUFFET *Dans le Rôle Prodigieux du Roi Assassin!"*

We see three doors in all. One leads to the bedroom, one to the kitchen, and the main one, already mentioned, which opens to reveal the staircase coming down from the ground floor. Beside this main door is an inter-communicating telephone on the wall, connecting with the front door outside.

It is late afternoon. Seated in the gilded throne is LETTICE, *holding aloft a large furry cat.*]

LETTICE: [*To the cat*] My name is Felina, Queen of Sorrows! I allow this handmaid to hold me so intimately only that she may admire me better. My eyes are the color of molten topaz. Many proud Toms have drowned themselves in Old Nile for love of them! My lot is tragedy. I was cast forth from my palace beside the tumbling cataract—imprisoned cruelly in a dungeon beneath the Earl's Court Road! I, who dined off crayfish and Numidian scallops, forced to eat squalid preparations out of cans—the Kitty-Crunch and Whiskas of Affliction.

[*The legs of* LOTTE SCHOEN *walk into view above, cross the window, and go up the steps to the front door.*]

No matter, I will endure all—and when the time is ripe, the whole world will see my triumphant restoration to the throne! Then all will perish who wounded me— their eyes scratched from their treasonous heads!

[*The buzzer of the Intercom sounds loudly.* LETTICE *starts, alarmed.*]

Who's that?

[*Hastily she rises and peers up cautiously at the legs on the front steps, holding the cat.*]

[*To the cat*] What do you think? Hard legs, yes? . . . Proud, cat-kicking legs, I'd say . . . I wouldn't trust them, would you?

[*The buzzer sounds again harshly, making her jump.*]

Oh, dear . . .

[*Nervously she goes to the Intercom by the door and lifts the phone.*]

[*Into it*] Yes? . . . Who is it, please?

[*The audience hears what* LETTICE *hears in her receiver, through speakers.*]

LOTTE: [*Brisk*] Miss Douffet?
LETTICE: [*Faintly*] Yes . . .
LOTTE: This is Miss Schoen.
LETTICE: Who?
LOTTE: Miss Schoen. From the Trust. Do you remember?

[LETTICE *stands aghast.*]

Hallo? . . . Miss Douffet? . . . Are you there?
LETTICE: [*In a whisper*] Yes . . .
LOTTE: Can you hear me? [*Insistent*] Miss Douffet? Can you hear me?
LETTICE: [*To the cat*] It's her . . . The Executioner!

[*The buzzer sounds again, imperiously.*]

[*Into the phone; louder*] Hallo?

LOTTE: Please let me in. I have to see you.

LETTICE: No!

LOTTE: It's just for a moment. You won't regret it, I assure you.

LETTICE: [*Faintly*] I don't choose . . . I really do not.

LOTTE: What are you saying? I can't hear you!

LETTICE: [*A little louder*] I do not choose to receive you. Please go away.

LOTTE: Miss Douffet, I do very much need to see you. Please let me in. [*Pause.*] Are you listening?

[*We see* LOTTE *crouching down and peering through the side window, trying to see in. She raps sharply on the railings with her umbrella.* LETTICE *shrinks back against the wall. The face disappears, and the buzzer goes again. And again. And again.*]

[*Raising her voice; sharply*] Miss Douffet, this is absurd! Please let me in at once!

[*A long blast on the buzzer.*]

Miss Douffet, I insist!

LETTICE: [*In distress*] Oh, dear . . . Very well!

[*She presses the button to release the catch on the front door and opens the one to her flat.*]

[*Calling up the stairs*] Enter if you must! Down to the dungeon!

[LOTTE's *legs disappear into the house.* LETTICE *stands rigid. We hear feet marching down the stairs and* LOTTE *appears.*]

LOTTE: Good afternoon. It is very good of you to see me. [*Seeing the cat in* LETTICE's *arms*] *Ah!*

[*She retreats in panic, half closing the door.*]

LETTICE: What is it?

LOTTE: A cat!

LETTICE: This is Felina.

LOTTE: I'm sorry, I can't come in! Not with that!

LETTICE: Why not?

LOTTE: Allergy. The doctor calls it that anyway. I know it's something deeper. Either way it prevents my entering.

LETTICE: She can be banished for five minutes.

LOTTE: I'd be grateful.

LETTICE: Very well.

[LETTICE *goes into the bedroom with Felina and returns alone, shutting the door. Cautiously* LOTTE *enters the flat.*]

[*Coldly*] She is confined in the shoe cupboard.

LOTTE: Thank you. That's most kind.

LETTICE: Not to her. She prefers being in here . . . What did you mean, something deeper than allergy?

LOTTE: I have an actual aversion to cats. Their sinuousness and slyness. I try to conquer it but can't. They actually make my throat swell.

LETTICE: Well, that's mutual. Felina's throat swells when she meets *people* she doesn't like. They are creatures of deep instinct, of course.

LOTTE: So I have been told.

LETTICE: Would you like to sit down?

[*She gestures to the wooden throne.*]

LOTTE: What an interesting chair. Was it one of your mother's?

LETTICE: How do you know that?

LOTTE: It looks rather like a prop.

LETTICE: That is her Falstaff chair. [LOTTE *looks at her, startled.*] You may occupy it if you like. [*Indicating the gilded chair*] Or you may take the endored one.

LOTTE: I wouldn't presume.

LETTICE: You have my assent.

LOTTE: Well . . . thank you.

[*She sits on the wooden one.* LETTICE *goes into the kitchen. An awkward pause.*]

[*Raising her voice.*] Miss Douffet, I hope my coming here is not disturbing for you.

LETTICE: Why should it be? After all, you have no powers here.

LOTTE: I beg your pardon?

[LETTICE *returns with a packet of dry cat food, which she pours into a bowl.*]

LETTICE: You have done all you can to me. I am quite beyond your jurisdiction.

LOTTE: My dear woman, I haven't come to *do* anything to you.

LETTICE: Don't! . . . Don't say that, please . . . I am not "dear" to you. I am not dear at all.

LOTTE: It was just a form of words.

LETTICE: I respect words.

LOTTE: So do I. Intensely.

LETTICE: Why have you come? To gloat? To look on my condition?

LOTTE: To see how you are, certainly.

LETTICE: Well, then, you see!—Behold!

LOTTE: You've been well?

LETTICE: I can't believe you're interested in that.

LOTTE: You have found some work, one hopes?

LETTICE: Does one?

LOTTE: Of course. I'm sure it's not easy.

LETTICE: Oh, yes! In my case—very!

LOTTE: Really?

LETTICE: Extremely, actually. [*Cold*] Since I saw you it has been, I think, ten weeks.

LOTTE: About that, yes.

LETTICE: In that period I have worked for *one . . .* I found employment in a large store on Oxford Street. In the food department during British Cheese Week. I had to dress up in a green crinoline and a pink muslin cap— and offer samples of a new cheese called Devon Dream. My week did not run its full course.

LOTTE: You left?

LETTICE: I was asked to leave.

LOTTE: I'm sorry. May I ask why?

LETTICE: I would rather not delve into it.

[*She goes into the bedroom with the bowl of cat food. A loud meow sends* LOTTE *in renewed panic over to the stairs.* LETTICE *comes back into the room to find her there with some surprise. She shuts the bedroom door and* LOTTE *cautiously returns to her chair.*]

LOTTE: Miss Douffet, to come to the point: Since we met, you have been somewhat on my conscience.

LETTICE: [*Coldly*] Really?

LOTTE: I am aware it is not easy for you—for us, people of our age and background—to find employment of any kind—let alone that which suits us . . . I have been keeping an eye open on your behalf.

LETTICE: How peculiar.

LOTTE: Peculiar?

LETTICE: To push someone in the gutter and then toy with pulling them out. Remorse, my mother used to say, is a useless emotion.

LOTTE: [*Stiffly*] It is hardly that, I can assure you. I was not remotely wrong in doing what I did. I would do it again. All the same, in a friendly spirit—I have been on the watch for you. That is all I'm saying. If it's of interest. [*A pause.*] I have actually discovered something you might enjoy doing. Should I go on?

LETTICE: [*Equally stiffly*] If you wish.

LOTTE: A married couple who live next door to me run a business of tourist boats on the Thames. The public embarks at Westminster Bridge and is addressed throughout by a guide using a microphone. I have been speaking to this couple, and they are badly in need of helpers: people who have enthusiasm for history—with particular regard to the river. I told them I knew exactly the person. I did somewhat exceed the limits of veracity—but if you were interested you could easily read up the subject—at least sufficiently not to make a liar out of me . . . You would of course have to swear to me absolutely that there would be no departures of any kind from the strictest historical truth. [*Pause.*] The pay is not enormous, but there are tips—this time legitimately sanctioned by the management—and these apparently can be generous. Also, of course, though I should not say it, they need not be declared . . . I have provided for you, on the notepaper of the Preservation Trust, a letter of reference, which could be useful in impressing my friends—and indeed other possible employers in the future. Would you care to see it?

LETTICE: If you would care to show it.

[LOTTE *takes the letter from her handbag and gives it to* LETTICE.]

[*Reading it aloud*] "This is to introduce Miss Douffet. Working as a guide for the Trust, Miss Douffet became a popular favorite with many members of the visiting public. During the last few months of her employment especially, they showed their appreciation of her particular style by writing many letters expressing gratitude. Besides an extensive knowledge of history, Miss Douffet specializes in an imaginative manner of narration essentially her own. One which ensures that any tour over which she presides becomes a veritably unforgettable experience . . . "

[*A long pause.* LETTICE *is very moved.*]

I have not deserved this.

LOTTE: Please.

LETTICE: No! Really! I have not . . . [*Increasingly upset*] I—I repaid your confidence with folly—and you reward me like this . . . It is out of all measure . . . You are—you are very good. Yes. You are a most good—a good—a very good—a good—Oh, *dear!*

[*She is over the brink of tears.*]

LOTTE: [*Alarmed*] Oh, please! Please, Miss Douffet!

LETTICE: I swear—I swear to you—if I can do this job, I shall not deviate by so much as a syllable from the recorded truth! . . . I shall read and read! I shall commit to memory every recorded fact about the river! I shall not depart from them by so much as one cedilla—not a jot or tittle! Not one iota!

LOTTE: [*Embarrassed*] Please, Miss Douffet!

[LETTICE *tears the property sword off the wall and kneels, holding it up ardently.*]

LETTICE: *I swear this!* . . . Not one complaint will you hear! Not a single—not a single—a sing—

[*Her tears overcome her again, more freely than before.* LOTTE *is horrified by the emotion shown.*]

LOTTE: Oh, please now! Please—Really, Miss Douffet! I beg you! Please! This is quite unnecessary . . . I'm only too glad to be of help! . . . *Please!* Really and truly, I can assure you—[*Wildly, as the sobs continue*] Do you possibly have a cup of tea? That would be so nice! A cup of strong hot tea . . . ?

LETTICE: [*Bewildered*] What?

LOTTE: Or coffee! Coffee would do! . . . Or Coca-Cola! I must admit to a fondness for Coca-Cola!

[LETTICE *stops sobbing and looks at her in disbelief.*]

LOTTE: But of course you wouldn't have that, would you?

[LETTICE *shakes her head: No.*]

Well, anything will do. A glass of plain water would be
delicious!

LETTICE: [*Recovering*] No! . . . *Quaff!*

LOTTE: What?

LETTICE: Quaff! That's its name. You must have quaff!

LOTTE: What's that?

LETTICE: Perfect . . . Just perfect for the occasion!

LOTTE: Quaff?

LETTICE: My cordial. Sixteenth century! . . . It's one of my
greatest hobbies: the food and drink of Tudor times.
Would you—could you possibly bear to sample it? I'd be
so delighted if you could! . . . Would you let me toast you
in it now?

LOTTE: [*Nervously*] I don't know . . . I drink very little.

LETTICE: Oh, yes, please! You must try it: it's very enlarging! When I am alone I do not dare to even sip it—it
makes me too full of song and story! . . . Say yes—please!

LOTTE: Well—just a *very* little.

LETTICE: I'll get it! [*She moves excitedly towards the
kitchen.*] It has stayed in the kitchen untasted for far
too long . . . We'll have it in goblets! I have two splendid
ones Mother used in the tavern scene in *Henry IV!*
. . . Take your coat off, I entreat it.

LOTTE: Thank you.

[LETTICE *disappears.* LOTTE *removes her coat. From
the kitchen we hear* LETTICE *singing the soldier's
drinking song from* Othello *("And let me the canni-
kin clink, clink!") in a jubilant voice. She reappears
carrying a tray with two theatrical goblets studded
with fake jewels and a strange home-gilded bottle of
liquor.*]

LETTICE: Here it is! Pour generously.

[*She sets down the tray and proffers the goblets to* LOTTE *who picks up the bottle and pours gingerly.*]

No, no, please—more! It is not meant to drip into the glass but to cascade! . . . That's better. And now we quaff! Which being interpreted means—knock it back! [*Toasting*] To you! . . . Of course you can't drink to yourself, so I'll just do it and then you can follow: "To Miss Schoen—a generous friend!" [*She swirls the liquor in the goblet.*] One—two—three—*Quaff!*

[*She swallows it, gasping delightedly.*]

LOTTE: Now it's my turn. "To Miss Douffet—who surprised me greatly!"

LETTICE: Oh, that's charming! [*Encouraging*] One—two—three—Quaff!

[LOTTE *dubiously swirls her goblet then swallows the drink—and gasps at its strength.* LETTICE *is delighted.*]

Enlarging, isn't it?

LOTTE: It certainly is . . . What on earth is in it?

LETTICE: The pleasure it offers is both herbal and verbal. That's my little riddle. [*Pause.*] I imagine I appear rather an alien person to you.

LOTTE: That is not all bad, I suspect.

LETTICE: Let us recharge.

LOTTE: Is that wise?

LETTICE: Absolutely. One is never sufficient.

LOTTE: Well, all right—if I can linger with it a little. Less quaff and more sip.

LETTICE: At your pleasure.

LOTTE: What is your first name?

LETTICE: Lettice.

LOTTE: That's pretty.

LETTICE: It comes from Laetitia—the Latin word for gladness. As a vegetable it is obviously one of God's mistakes—but as a name it passes, I think.

LOTTE: Indeed. [*Toasting*] To Lettice!

LETTICE: [*Shyly*] Thank you ... What's yours? No—don't answer. Let me play the interviewer for once: you be the victim.

LOTTE: I don't think that's a very good idea.

LETTICE: Why not? It'll be a game! Imagine you are looking for employment and I'm the woman at the agency. In front of me is an enormous desk, covered with details of jobs—for none of which you're suitable. That's what they always imply anyway. [*Stern voice*] "Sit down, please, Miss—er, Schoen, isn't it?"

LOTTE: Correct.

[*She sits.* LETTICE *sits too, severely. They face each other, seated on the two thrones.*]

LETTICE: What is your first name?

LOTTE: Charlotte.

LETTICE: Charlotte Schoen. Hardly an English name.

LOTTE: No, my father was German.

LETTICE: But your mother was English?

LOTTE: Correct.

LETTICE: Of honest yeoman stock?

LOTTE: I don't know about that. She worked for the Home Office.

LETTICE: And your father: What was his work?

LOTTE: He published art books. The Perseus Press.

LETTICE: Oh, good heavens! He owned that?

LOTTE: You know it?

LETTICE: Very well! They are ravishing, those Perseus books! There's one in particular on the Baroque that is absolutely exquisite. It makes one almost swoon with delight.

LOTTE: That is entirely wrong, I'm afraid.

LETTICE: Is it?

LOTTE: Well, of course! Officials in employment agencies don't swoon.

LETTICE: I suppose they don't.

LOTTE: You have to show far more reserve than that.

LETTICE: How silly of me. Forgive me . . . *(The Interviewer again)* What was your education, please?

LOTTE: St. Paul's School for Girls. Then the Regency Street Polytechnic, for architecture.

LETTICE: You studied to be an architect?

LOTTE: Correct.

LETTICE: And qualified?

LOTTE: I'm afraid not. My mother ran off with someone in her office. After that my father became ill and needed me. The business was sold for far too little. We moved out of a large house in Kensington, into a small flat in Putney. I became more and more his nurse.

LETTICE: I'm sorry.

LOTTE: No need to be. He was worth it. He gave me a unique childhood.

LETTICE: Surrounded by art books on every civilization!

LOTTE: Yes. We had an enormous library where I virtually lived. At one end there was a huge window of colored glass—emerald and gold.

LETTICE: How lovely!

LOTTE: It's still there. Last week I walked by and there was a girl looking out of it with a completely shaven head, except for three spikes of green hair standing straight up like ice-cream cones.

LETTICE: Marie Antoinette would have loved that.

LOTTE: She would?

LETTICE: Oh, yes! She used to wear the most elaborate styles on her own head. Great ships at anchor on a sea of tossing curls! . . . I didn't invent that.

[LOTTE *looks at her severely.*]

LOTTE: I hope you are not one of those people who see good in anything—no matter how grotesque.

LETTICE: As Christians we are surely meant to perceive good wherever we can.

LOTTE: I am not a Christian, and the only good I perceive is in beauty . . . This world gets uglier by the minute, that's all I perceive for sure. I used to love the walls of our house: that cream stucco so characteristic of London. Now they are completely defaced with slogans. One says, "Hang the bloody Pope." Another says, "Hang the bloody Prots."

LETTICE: I can't read the writing on the walls around us. It's all in Arabic.

LOTTE: I wouldn't feel too deprived. I'm sure it's only saying hang someone else.

LETTICE: I just know it's all done by Mr. Pachmani.

LOTTE: Who is that?

LETTICE: My neighbor upstairs. Obviously a political conspirator . . . I just know he slinks out at night with a paint can and brush, looking for new walls to conquer.

LOTTE: In his country they'd cut off hands for that. Perhaps we should do the same.

LETTICE: How astounding that would be! A punishment straight out of *Titus Andronicus!* Aaron the Moor wields the axe—and the defacer's hand is rendered powerless for ever! I've always thought offenders should have the word "Vandal" sprayed on their foreheads with indelible paint—but your sentence is far more Shakespearian!

LOTTE: This entire city is actually crammed with fanatics from all over the globe fighting medieval crusades on our ground. Isn't it time we became a little fanatical ourselves on its behalf? . . . People in the past would not have endured it. But, of course, they had spunk. There's no one left now with any spunk at all.

LETTICE: Just the Mere! The Mere People! That's all who remain.

LOTTE: Ghosts! They're the worst! That's what we must never become ourselves—you and I. Not that there's much danger of it in your case.

LETTICE: Ghosts?

LOTTE: Gentlewomen who live in the past and wring their hands. My office is filled with them. Wring, wring, wring—all day long. [*Genteel voice*] "Oh, my goodness! Oh, what have we come to? Oh, this dreadful modern age!" . . . They should all be selling fragrant cushions in our gift shops! Or Tudor House tea towels! . . . I'm taking a course at this moment. Computers—processors—the whole modern thing. [*Accusingly*] How are you on all that?

LETTICE: Not expert, I must confess. I prefer the world of the handmade. The world of Quaff and Conversation.

LOTTE: [*Who is beginning to feel its influence*] Well, I
have to admit the quaff is surprisingly good—once one
gets used to it. [*She toasts* LETTICE, *who responds.*] Is
it really sixteenth century? One can hardly believe it.

LETTICE: An adaptation. By me. I regard it as an *hom-
mage,* as the French say. My bow to Tudor times.

LOTTE: And you're not saying what's in it?

LETTICE: [*Teasingly*] Both herbal and verbal! . . .

LOTTE: Well, one thing I can tell—it's extremely strong.

LETTICE: Naturally. Our ancestors possessed strong stom-
achs. Remember Falstaff! *He* wasn't Mere, was he? He
was the absolute antithesis of the Mere! . . . Let's have
a toast to him! My favorite character in all drama!

LOTTE: Really?

LETTICE: Certainly! The ton of man, fat as butter! Who's
yours?

LOTTE: I think I told you I don't share your passion for the
drama. In fact, I despise it. However one does admire
spunk. So—to Falstaff!

LETTICE: Falstaff! The old bed-presser!

[LOTTE *looks startled. They both drink.*]

LOTTE: Did your mother actually play that part herself?

LETTICE: Many times! He was her most successful role—
after Richard III. She virtually wore the same costume
for both. It was merely a matter of turning the pillow
round she used as a hump, from the back to the front.
[*Patting her stomach and rumbling*] "Holla! Maîtresse
Quickly! *Holla!*". . . It was utterly convincing. I remember she had beautiful white whiskers, and her cheeks
would glow like port-lamps on an ocean liner.

LOTTE: There was obviously nothing mere about her either. What was her watchword again?

LETTICE: "Enlarge! Enliven! Enlighten!"

LOTTE: Splendid! . . . Here's to her! Your mother!

[*She drinks.*]

LETTICE: [*Pleased*] Thank you.

LOTTE: She's not still performing, by any chance?

LETTICE: Ah, no. She died from a heart attack six years ago—onstage, playing Marc Antony in *Julius Caesar*. She was always rather too vigorous in the Forum Scene . . . Still, she went as she always wished—in harness. She used to say, "When my time comes, I want to go in a second. None of those nasty French nursing homes for me. Three-day-old croissants and wine you can run a car on!"

LOTTE: She was quite right. The Gallic spirit thrives on parsimony.

LETTICE: Tell me, is your father departed also?

LOTTE: Oh, yes.

LETTICE: I drink to him anyway! I'm sure he was not one of your ghosts.

LOTTE: Well, there, alas, you are wrong, my dear. That, I am afraid, is exactly what he *was.* Or at least became . . . It was inevitable, actually. He came from Dresden as a refugee. He used to say it was the most beautiful city on earth. Then in the war the Allies burnt it to the ground defending civilization. He never got over that. He died with Europe really.

LETTICE: Europe?

LOTTE: That's the only thing that sustained him—his love for Europe. I mean the actual buildings. The towns and villages of five hundred years. All virtually destroyed in five. [*Pause.*] He believed anybody born after 1940 has no real idea what visual civilization means—and never can have. "There used to be such a thing as the Communal Eye," he'd say. "It has been put out in our lifetime, Lotte—yours and mine! The disgusting world we live in now could simply not have been built when that eye was open. The planners would have been torn limb from limb—not given knighthoods!"

LETTICE: Oh, how right! How absolutely *right!* . . . I wish I'd known him!

LOTTE: Yes, well, I'm his daughter—and that's the whole trouble.

LETTICE: What do you mean?

LOTTE: Because I have his eyes. It's all he left me, and I don't want them. I wish I was blind, like everyone else.

LETTICE: Don't say that!

LOTTE: I mean it! All I am now is a freak. I have *his* disease, only worse. I care—I actually care more for buildings than their inhabitants. When I imagine Dresden burning, all I see are those exquisite shapes of the Baroque—domes, pediments, golden cherubs going up in flames. Not people at all, just beautiful shapes vanishing for ever . . . I'm an idolator. That's what my friend called me, and he was right . . . If I could save a great Baroque city or its people I would choose the city every time. People come again: cities never.

LETTICE: Who was that you mentioned—your friend?

LOTTE: A fellow student at the Polytechnic. Jim Mackintosh. An industrial chemist. Quite remarkably handsome.

LETTICE: [*Obligingly pouring more quaff into* LOTTE'S

goblet] That's exceptional, I'd say. They don't tend much to go in for beauty, do they, chemists?

LOTTE: His hair was pure gold. When I first met him I thought he dyed it, it was so startlingly bright—but he didn't. He was known in college as the Blond Bombshell. Very appropriate, actually.

LETTICE: What do you mean?

LOTTE: We used to walk through the city endlessly together, watching it be destroyed. That was the true Age of Destruction—the late fifties and sixties. You realize the British destroyed London ultimately, not the Germans. There would be gangs of workmen all over the place, bashing down our heritage. Whole terraces of Georgian buildings crashing to the ground. I still see those great balls of iron swinging against elegant façades—street after street! All those fanlights shattering—enchanting little doorways—perfectly proportioned windows, bash bash bash!—and no one stopping it. It was exactly like being hit oneself. One day watching, I actually threw up in the street . . . That was when I said to him, "Do it."

LETTICE: Do what?

LOTTE: Nothing. I'm talking too much. This stuff makes one babble.

[*She slams down her goblet.*]

LETTICE: Please don't stop. What did you mean, "Do it"?

[*A pause.*]

LOTTE: Something I'd talked to him about before. One night standing on the South Bank of the Thames outside the Shell Building. It was nearly finished: a great dead weight of Not Trying. Not Trying and Not Caring! I remember I was so angry looking at it, I said, "The people who put this up should be hanged in public for debauching the public imagination!"

LETTICE: *Bravo!*

LOTTE: And then I said—"Why should all the bombs just fall on beauty? Why shouldn't one at least be used on ugliness—purely as protest? Witness that someone at least still has eyes!"

LETTICE: Gracious!

LOTTE: After all, we all have to live with it. We all have to endure it forever! Why are we all so *tame?* . . . If we really cared, we would blow this up! [*More and more excited*] We would go around in secret and destroy this kind of awfulness, *all* these excrescences, anywhere we saw we had to! We'd blow these things into bits as soon as they were finished—till builders were afraid to put them up!—no, no—till architects were afraid to design them! That would make a statement in the world for all to see! . . . I said we should call ourselves the End. E.N.D. The Eyesore Negation Detachment!

[LETTICE *claps.*]

Jim just looked at me—his eyes were shining. He had a great deal of Scottish passion buried inside him . . . And then do you know what he said? "A bomb is very easy to make."

[*A long pause, during which* LETTICE *solemnly hands* LOTTE *the jug.* LOTTE *pours herself another large drink and imbibes it, deeply.*]

LETTICE: [*Breathlessly*] Go on.

LOTTE: Well, when I said, "Do it"—he did it.

LETTICE: Made a bomb?

LOTTE: Two. One for each wing of the Shell Building. He was brilliant at science. While he was making them I was studying the site. You wouldn't believe how easy it was in the days before terrorism to get into a building still under construction. All it took was a cap and over-alls—and in my case a false mustache.

LETTICE: [*Delighted*] You dressed up as a workman?

LOTTE: Exactly. I looked very convincing. Jim explained to me over and over how to activate my bomb, and then we took them in separate taxis, hidden in toolbags. I took the right wing, he took the left. It reflected our politics! . . . We decided to leave them in separate lavatories on the first floor. They were timed to explode together at four in the morning, long before anyone got to work.

[*A pause.*]

LETTICE: And?

LOTTE: [*Embarrassed*] Well . . . he put *his* into the build-ing, and I didn't . . . I got cold feet at the last moment. Instead I dropped mine into the river, off Waterloo Bridge . . . Next morning we listened together in bed to the six o'clock news. There was nothing about any explosion. Nor on the seven, nor the eight. His obvi-ously hadn't gone off. Now we were in the most dread-ful position! Workmen were there all day long—what if it exploded when people were there? . . . He said, "We must return at once and fetch them out!" And so then I had to confess—there was only one to fetch. He didn't

say anything. Just went straight out and collected it—
and brought it back home. He dismantled it in front of
me on the kitchen table, in dead silence . . . That wasn't
all he dismantled.

LETTICE: What do you mean?

LOTTE: Well, *us*, of course. He dismantled us as well. He
looked at me with total contempt. As if I'd betrayed
him. Which of course I had.

LETTICE: No!

LOTTE: Absolutely! I'd proposed the whole thing, then
run out on him behind his back. If anything had gone
wrong he would have had to take the whole blame . . .
We split up within days after that.

LETTICE: I'm so sorry.

LOTTE: [*Protesting*] I was *frightened* . . . I didn't want to
get caught!

LETTICE: Of course not! That's understandable . . . He
should have understood that!

LOTTE: [*Harshly*] Nonsense! Why should he? It was cow-
ardly and deserved entirely what it got . . . Entirely.

[*A pause.* LOTTE *glares.*]

LETTICE: Where is he now? Do you ever . . . see him?

LOTTE: He found a job abroad. Ironically enough with the
Shell Company. A thorough waste, I thought. He was
too original for that. [*Pause.*] We both wasted ourselves
in the end.

LETTICE: That's not true.

LOTTE: Absolutely.

LETTICE: Why? You have a wonderful job! Everything
you could wish for! . . . I know you could have been an

architect—but that was just unlucky. Your father need-
ing you, and having to give up your studies.

LOTTE: [*Stiffly*] That was not the reason. I lost interest
after Jim left—and failed my exams.

LETTICE: Oh, dear.

LOTTE: One deserves everything one gets in this world.
In my case, the desk.

LETTICE: Desk?

LOTTE: Where I sit now. Among the ghosts . . . The Non-
doer's Desk.

LETTICE: That's not fair. You do things!

LOTTE: Hire and fire. How courageous.

LETTICE: You are very hard on yourself.

LOTTE: [*Tartly*] Oh, stop it! There's no point babbling on
about it. I can't imagine why I started. It was all a long
time ago, and disgraceful then!

LETTICE: No!

LOTTE: Stupid, dangerous, and childish. If I hadn't been
driven into indiscretion by this brew of yours, I would
never have told you.

[*She glares at her. A pause.*]

LETTICE: I'm glad you did.

LOTTE: Well . . . I really must go now. [*Gathering up her
things*] I wish you luck with the tour boat—and if
there's anything you want, don't hesitate to telephone.
[*She sways dizzily.*] Oh, good gracious!

LETTICE: What's the matter?

LOTTE: Nothing. I'm fine.

LETTICE: Is it one of your headaches?

LOTTE: No. It's one too many of your drinks!

LETTICE: Oh, dear!

LOTTE: Don't worry. I'll be perfectly all right once I've had some food.

LETTICE: Let me get you some. I could make you a tansy in no time at all. That's a medieval omelette.

LOTTE: Oh, no, really! [*She produces her bottle of cologne, shakes some on to her handkerchief and applies it to her temples.*] Just tell me what on earth you put in that drink—and without the riddle, please.

LETTICE: It's nothing dangerous, I assure you. Just mead, vodka, sugar, and lovage.

LOTTE: Lovage? What's that?

LETTICE: Lovage. A herb. Its name derives from "love" and "ache." "Ache" is the medieval word for parsley.

LOTTE: You really are a unique person, Lettice. If I were you, I'd bottle it and sell it in one of those gourmet shops. You could have your own little stall.

LETTICE: Just so long as I don't have to wear a crinoline and a muslin cap.

LOTTE: Tell me—what exactly did you do in that shop on Oxford Street to get you fired? When you had to sell that British cheese.

LETTICE: Devon Dream? Well, it was unsalable! It was bright tangerine and tasted of saddle soap. I *tried* to sell it. I'm afraid I used methods you would not approve.

LOTTE: [*Dryly*] Ah.

LETTICE: I informed the public it was the most historical of all British cheeses—famous throughout the fifteenth century for its medicinal properties. I even went on to add it was tried as a remedy by Richard the Third, who ate a pound of it every day for a month in the hope of reducing his hump.

LOTTE: You didn't!

LETTICE: Desperate moments demand desperate measures! . . . Anyway it didn't do me any good: I failed to sell a single slice. Finally I just told them they could make a much better cheese at home for half the price, and gave them a superb recipe from the year sixteen-hundred, involving rosewater and radishes. They were all delighted—except the Manager, who told me to get out! That man is an absolute churl deluxe.

[*A pause.* LOTTE *looks at* LETTICE.]

LOTTE: Would you do me a favour? Would you dine with me? I'm a member of the Palladian Club. It's for professional people connected with architecture. The food you will find extremely *mere,* but it has the advantage of being close by, in Holland Park.

LETTICE: [*Overwhelmed*] Well, really—I don't know what to say. That is most kind, most kind indeed . . . if you mean it.

LOTTE: I don't say what I don't mean.

LETTICE: I—haven't got a really appropriate dress.

LOTTE: There isn't such a thing in this case.

LETTICE: I could wear my cloak over this. It's decent black, as they say.

LOTTE: Your Mary Queen of Scots cloak?

LETTICE: Yes.

LOTTE: I must say as long as I live I shall not forget that moment in my office. Did you make that garment yourself?

LETTICE: Yes—for my mother. It was Lady Macbeth's nightdress.

LOTTE: To be truthful, it was really what made me come here today.

LETTICE: The nightdress?

LOTTE: The uniqueness . . . After you left I looked up the story you told about the Queen. It was every word true.

[*A pause.*]

LETTICE: Did you doubt it?

LOTTE: Well, you *have* been known to improve on history.

LETTICE: I told you—only when it needs it. That story doesn't. It's perfect. Do you know how it ended?

LOTTE: With her death, I presume.

LETTICE: Not at all. There was more. She had the very last laugh! [*Gleefully*] It was the custom after decapitating someone for the executioner to hold up the severed head to the crowd and say, "So perish all the Queen's enemies!" Mary anticipated that—just as with the dress. She had put on for the occasion a wig of auburn hair. No one had seen her for years, so most of the onlookers didn't know it was not her own. When the headsman stooped to pick up the head, he was left clutching a handful of beautiful fair curls! The head just stayed where it was on the ground— displaying to all what she had suffered during those endless years of captivity. A skull of little cropped gray hairs . . . That is the true end of the scene, and certainly does not need improvement.

LOTTE: Absolutely not.

LETTICE: Excuse me. I'll get my cloak.

[*She goes into the bedroom.* LOTTE *is left alone, looking wonderingly after her. A pause. She goes to the table, picks up her goblet, and drains it—then unex-*

pectedly picks up the other one and drains that too to give her courage. Finally she walks around to the far side of the gilded chair and suddenly—inexplicably—drops to her knees by the golden throne, facing out front. LETTICE *returns, wearing her black cloak, to find* LOTTE *in this position.*]

[*Alarmed*] Oh, dear! What is it? Are you ill? . . . You're ill, aren't you?—and it's my fault! Oh, dear, dear, dear—I've made you ill!

LOTTE: [*Calmly*] Come here.

LETTICE: I'm sorry.

LOTTE: Come here.

[*Hesitantly* LETTICE *approaches the kneeling figure.*]

Now pull . . . [*She lowers her head.*] Don't be shy, just pull.

[*Tentatively* LETTICE *extends her hand to* LOTTE's *head.*]

Go on. Be brave.

[LETTICE *touches* LOTTE's *hair and then pulls it. It comes away in her hand: it is a wig. Beneath it is revealed a head of fluffy gray hair.*]

[*Shyly*] So perish all the Queen's enemies!

[*A pause.* LETTICE *is overcome with amazement. She holds up the wig in delight.*]

LETTICE: Oh, wonderful, wonderful! *Wonderful—beyond measure!*

[*A pause.*]

Please—have dinner just like that.

LOTTE: [*Shy*] Really?

LETTICE: Oh, *yes!* . . . I never saw anything that needed improving less! . . . Honestly.

[LOTTE *takes her hand and rises.*]

LOTTE: Very well . . . I will.

[*They look at each other. Then* LETTICE *laughs, a clear bright laugh of perception, and walks away across the room. She laughs again.*]

What is it? What are you thinking?

[*But instead of replying,* LETTICE *takes off her black cloak and lays it ceremoniously at the base of the staircase, in the manner of Sir Walter Raleigh assisting Queen Elizabeth.*]

LETTICE: Come, madam. Your hedgehogs await!

[*Sumptuous music sounds.* LOTTE, *entranced, walks with an attempt at grandeur across the room, over the cloak, and up the stairs. The curtain falls.*]

END OF ACT II

ACT THREE

[Lettice's flat. Six months later. Again late afternoon.

The room is in some disarray. The front door has clearly been smashed in and hangs precariously against the wall, exposing the dingy staircase outside, descending from the hall above. The bedroom door is closed. One new object is a large square shape covered with a black shawl.

In the Falstaff chair, sitting quite inappropriately, is MR. BARDOLPH, *a solicitor. He is a middle-aged lawyer, dry, and professional.* LETTICE *stands looking up out of the window. There is a silence between them, which has obviously been of some duration. Outside a nearby clock strikes four.]*

BARDOLPH: I am waiting, Miss Douffet. I hope, patiently. My patience, however, is not inexhaustible. Nor is my time. I ask you again, will you now speak to me? Plainly and clearly? . . . Well?

LETTICE: *[Turning]* I really don't think you should have come here, Mr. Bardolph.

BARDOLPH: I would much have preferred to interview you at my office. I did suggest that, if you recall.

LETTICE: I really feel I have a right to my privacy, criminal though it may be, in the eyes of the police. I had always assumed that being granted bail meant also being granted that. Evidently I was wrong.

BARDOLPH: My dear Miss Douffet, how can I possibly make you understand—?

LETTICE: *Please!* Do not use that form of words to me. I am not your "dear." We have only met once before, please to remember.

BARDOLPH: I am fully aware of it—and a most unsatisfactory meeting it was. You told me nothing whatever.

LETTICE: I seem to recall you counseled silence.

BARDOLPH: To the police: not to me! I am—at least I am under the impression that I am—representing you, Miss Douffet. [*Sarcastic*] Or am I mistaken?

LETTICE: My assistance will come from other quarters.

BARDOLPH: You mean you have engaged another lawyer behind my back?

LETTICE: No.

BARDOLPH: Then from whom will it come? From what other quarters?

LETTICE: I would prefer to remain silent.

BARDOLPH: This is unbelievable. Do you actually realize the situation you are in? You are charged by the police with a peculiarly unpleasant crime. You go to trial in less than five weeks, and you tell me nothing with which one can possibly help you . . . I have nothing to go on—nothing to send to counsel! It is actually impossible for a solicitor to act for a client under such conditions!

LETTICE: Please do not distress yourself, Mr. Bardolph. All will be made plain at the proper time.

BARDOLPH: By whom? When and where made plain?

LETTICE: In court. In the dock. By Miss Schoen.

BARDOLPH: *Miss Schoen?!*

LETTICE: She is, as the Bible says, my shield and my buckler.

BARDOLPH: I don't actually believe I'm hearing *any* of this . . . She is *what?*

LETTICE: My defense, in whom I rest. Is that such an obscure word for a lawyer to understand—defense?

BARDOLPH: [*Controlling himself*] Miss Douffet: It may have escaped your notice that the lady you mention is not appearing in your defense. She is a prosecution witness—*against* you. In fact, she is the main witness against you.

LETTICE: [*Loftily*] That is impossible. She will speak and all will be clarified.

BARDOLPH: But she has already spoken. The police interviewed her in the hospital, and it is obviously on her statement alone that there is a case to answer. We are dealing with an extremely grave offense. You are charged with attempted murder. It is somewhat unlikely that your victim will speak in your defense. Victims on the whole do not tend to do that . . . Now I would much appreciate it if you would speak yourself. Forthwith!

[*A pause.*]

LETTICE: What exactly did she say? I demand to know what she said against me!

BARDOLPH: That you struck her with an axe.

LETTICE: And nothing else?

BARDOLPH: That really is quite sufficient for the police.

LETTICE: She said I assaulted her?

BARDOLPH: Apparently, yes.

LETTICE: And nothing else?

BARDOLPH: As far as I know.

[*A pause.*]

LETTICE: [*In sudden distress*] I have been betrayed . . .
Utterly betrayed! History repeats itself forever!

BARDOLPH: What are you saying?

LETTICE: Nothing! . . . I cannot believe it! She would
never do this to me! She is the soul of honesty. Honesty
and accuracy are her watchwords!

BARDOLPH: All I know is that they have brought a case on
her assertion—and you have to answer it.

LETTICE: I left a message on her telephone answering
machine. I said you would be coming here. I am not
adept at such devices, but she will understand it all the
same. She will come here herself and explain everything—you'll see. She'll come to my rescue! She'll throw
the accusation back at you as deep as to the lungs!

[BARDOLPH *stands up.*]

BARDOLPH: [*Losing his patience*] Miss Douffet—I am
making no accusation of *her!* It is *you* who are the
accused—and you stand in peril of going to prison for
a considerable time if you don't let me help you! Now—
for the last time—will you speak to me or not? Otherwise I will recommend another solicitor and leave you.

[*A pause. He reaches for his briefcase.*]

LETTICE: If she has borne false witness and delivered me
into the hands of jailers—then so be it.

BARDOLPH: That means yes? [*Pause: impatiently*] That means yes, Miss Douffet?

LETTICE: [*Exploding*] *Yes!* . . . *YES!*

BARDOLPH: Good.

LETTICE: I have deserved better of her. I truly have . . . [*Defiant*] Ask your questions, Mr. Bardolph! I will speak everything.

BARDOLPH: Thank you . . . I will recapitulate the facts and you will correct me wherever necessary. I shall record our conversation, if you don't mind.

[*He produces a tape recorder from the case.* LETTICE *sits in the gilded chair.*]

LETTICE: Must you?

BARDOLPH: It makes for accuracy.

LETTICE: As you will.

BARDOLPH: Turn it on yourself, when you are ready.

[*He places it on the table beside her. But* LETTICE *has no idea how to turn it on. She makes a stab at it but fails—pressing the eject button instead, so that the little door opens. With weary patience,* BARDOLPH *closes it and starts it for her.*]

There. [*He sits.*] Now: You are Lettice Douffet?

LETTICE: [*Putting her mouth very close to the machine*] Correct.

BARDOLPH: On Wednesday the thirty-first of January this year, Police Constable Harris, attached to the Earl's Court Road station—

LETTICE: The thirtieth.

BARDOLPH: I'm sorry?

LETTICE: On the *thirtieth* of January. That's most important.

BARDOLPH: On the thirtieth of January, Police Constable Harris was passing outside this house: number 19 Rastridge Road. He heard a cry, which made him look down into the basement area through your window. *That* window, I take it.

LETTICE: Correct.

BARDOLPH: He saw two figures—subsequently identified as yourself and Miss Charlotte Schoen. Miss Schoen was lying on the floor with blood pouring out of a deep cut in her head. You were standing over her, holding an axe.

LETTICE: Correct.

BARDOLPH: The constable ran up the steps and rang your bell. But you did not admit him.

LETTICE: Correct.

BARDOLPH: He rang all the bells in the house until admitted by the tenant of the flat immediately above here. A Mr. Pachmeen—

LETTICE: [*Venomously*] Pachmani.

BARDOLPH: The constable then rushed downstairs and banged violently on your door, but no one answered. Finally he had to break down the door.

LETTICE: As you see. Since I lack the money to repair it, I am now at the total mercy of every marauder in London. Including Mr. Pachmani, who is unquestionably violent and almost certainly making plans upstairs at this very minute to overthrow several governments.

BARDOLPH: Just keep to the facts, please. What happened next?

LETTICE: The policeman crashed into my room.

BARDOLPH: And arrested you?

LETTICE: Yes.

BARDOLPH: Go on.

LETTICE: He called an ambulance for Lotte on Mr. Pach-

mani's telephone, then apparently summoned help.
Obviously, he found himself unable to deal with me
alone. I am so formidable, you see. Two more police-
men arrived almost immediately and pinioned me.

BARDOLPH: Pinioned?

LETTICE: Each grasped an arm and led me through a
thicket of goggling neighbors into a waiting car. It was
deeply humiliating.

BARDOLPH: You were taken to a police station?

LETTICE: And hurled into a cell.

BARDOLPH: *Hurled?*

LETTICE: Led—with brusqueness.

BARDOLPH: And then?

LETTICE: I was shown a list of solicitors whom I could
consult.

BARDOLPH: For legal aid?

LETTICE: Not having a disposable income of more than
fifty pounds a week, I apparently qualify for free help.

BARDOLPH: And what made you choose me?

LETTICE: Your name. Bardolph. The merry companion to
Falstaff. [*Pause.*] Names can be misleading . . . The rest
I think you know.

BARDOLPH: You were taken to a magistrates' court the
next day and later released on bail when it was understood that the victim was not dangerously hurt . . . Now,
Miss Douffet: We come to the difficult bit. Apparently
Mr. Pachmani told the police that violent noises frequently emanated from this flat. He is no doubt pre-
pared to swear to this in the witness box.

LETTICE: [*Scornfully*] What sort of noises does he say—
emanated?

BARDOLPH: Cries. Bumps. Voices raised in fury and
sometimes apparently in screaming and pleading. He is

emphatic about this. He says such quarrels were a constant accompaniment to his evenings.

LETTICE: With his ears pressed to the floorboards, no doubt.

BARDOLPH: [*Testily*] I do not know the position of his ears. I do know that he has said he would rather forfeit his chance of Paradise than spend another winter living—as he put it—above those two demented female infidels.

LETTICE: [*Rising, outraged*] He says what?! ... The smirking, sneering Ottomite!

BARDOLPH: And that he will bear witness in the Crown Court that you and Miss Schoen fought continually, with violence. Now—is this true?

[*A pause.*]

LETTICE: Yes. In a way.

BARDOLPH: In what way? ... Miss Douffet, please go on. I have to know what happened in this room.

[*A long pause.*]

LETTICE: Executions.

BARDOLPH: I beg your pardon?

LETTICE: Executions.

[*A pause.*]

BARDOLPH: Could you elaborate?

LETTICE: Miss Schoen and I became acquainted six months ago when she was instrumental in finding me work as a tour guide on a London riverboat. A task, I may say, which I performed to universal satisfaction. One American actually declared that in a lifetime of tourism he had never before encountered such a combination of romantic fire with total factual accuracy. I even managed cunningly, as we sailed, to distract my listeners from seeing the nastier examples of modern buildings which now shamefully disfigure our historic waterway. When we docked at Westminster pier I would place a midshipman's cap by the gangplank to receive any tokens the voyagers might care to leave me. That cap *brimmed*, Mr. Bardolph! It literally cascaded with the currency of gratitude!

BARDOLPH: I am extremely glad to hear that, Miss Douffet. Could you, however, contrive to keep to the main thread of your narrative? You were speaking of your relationship with Miss Schoen.

LETTICE: Well, as a result of this nautical triumph, our friendship flowered. It transpired that we both harboured an enthusiasm for the heroic figures of the Past. People of spunk, as she would say. Especially those whose distinction earned them death at the hands of the Mere. I have always been fascinated by the way such people met their ends: the pride and grandeur of the world now gone . . . As we got to know each other better, we came more and more to sit upon the ground, as Shakespeare has it, and tell sad stories of the deaths of kings. Not just kings, of course: men and women of all conditions with regal hearts . . . In the end—entirely at my instigation, I don't deny it—we [*Pause*]—we came not only to tell the sad stories but to represent them.

BARDOLPH: [*Puzzled*] Represent?

LETTICE: Recall in Show how a few monumental spirits turned History into Legend . . . The fact that our country no longer produces such moments is, in our view, its gravest indictment. Laughable to you, no doubt, Mr. Bardolph. But then lawyers and legends have little in common.

[BARDOLPH *stares at her, beginning to be helplessly fascinated.*]

Miss Schoen herself had to be vigorously persuaded, I admit it freely. She loathed the theatrical in all forms— at least, so she protested. However, I soon perceived she protested altogether too much. In this room I watched her perform one small but thrilling act which could have only been ventured by someone longing in her heart to do what her tongue denounced . . . In an equally small way I was able to gratify that longing.

[*A pause.*]

BARDOLPH: Let me get this absolutely clear, please. Are you saying that you persuaded Miss Schoen to act out with you the deaths of famous women from the past?

LETTICE: Not just their deaths: That would make for a very short evening. Their trials as well. And not just women—there are simply not enough of them. We would choose a different subject each week—Mary Queen of Scots—Sir Walter Raleigh—King Charles I. We would read up separately everything we could about their last days—and then together explore their fate on Friday nights. She would come here or I would go to her: She has a flat in Putney, entirely lined with books of the Perseus Press . . . What was delightful was to see her change while playing—from embarrassment to excitement . . . Of course she is not an actress: She would be the first to agree with that. I myself inherited acting blood from my mother: Miss Schoen inherited more Civil Service blood from hers. Her parts tended therefore to be mainly those of Inquisitors. And of course she would also play all the Executioners—swinging the axe, working the guillotine and so forth.

BARDOLPH: [*Startled*] Guillotine?

LETTICE: Oh, yes. We didn't just keep to the confines of Britain. I have extensive connections with France. Miss Schoen disapproved of that country, but I managed to persuade her that French heroines tend to display more spectacular aspects of spunk than British. Marie Antoinette, for example, at bay before her judges.

BARDOLPH: May I ask how exactly you managed for a guillotine?

LETTICE: An old-fashioned blackboard and easel. You just pull out the pegs and down it comes. You have to get out of the way in time, of course.

BARDOLPH: Somewhat dangerous, I would say.

LETTICE: Without danger, Mr. Bardolph, there is no theater!

BARDOLPH: Did you dress up for these evenings?

LETTICE: Of course. For Marie Antoinette I had an excellent costume already from a former job connected with dairy produce: a green crinoline and a pink muslin cap. The cap in particular is an excellent touch. It gives me a striking resemblance to that wonderful sketch made by David as she was trundled by him on her way to execution. Do you know it?

BARDOLPH: I'm afraid not.

> [MISS SCHOEN's *legs are seen to march across the window and up the steps. She lets herself in the front door; the legs disappear.*]

LETTICE: It makes a most moving impression when I wear it in the court—standing in the prisoner's dock, one strand of hair escaping from it! Hair, of course, which used to be dressed in the most elaborate styles in all Europe . . . That was her finest hour, poor queen, her ordeal in court. Did you know she was accused of unnatural sexual practice?

BARDOLPH: I certainly didn't.

LETTICE: Oh, yes. Miss Schoen is dazzling as the prosecutor leveling that charge. She fairly spits it at me!—"Citizeness!" She snarls: "Citizeness! Do you deny that in your insatiable search for sensation you even enjoyed relations with your own *son?*"

[Lotte*'s legs are seen descending the staircase at the back. She comes through the broken door unobserved—slipping the keys of the flat into her bag—and stands listening behind* LETTICE, *her head elaborately bandaged, growing increasingly angry.*]

[*Acting it for the hypnotized* BARDOLPH] I stand as one numb! A hiss of horror fills the courtroom! Then slowly I raise my head up to the gallery, crammed with the vilest creatures in all Paris. My voice faltering but clearly audible—"I appeal," I say, "to every mother in this room! Do I need to answer such abomination?" . . . All stare down in wonder. Few can forbear to weep. Tears are seen, trickling down the leathery cheeks of fishwives! . . . I can tell you Lotte is absolutely glorious as an awestruck fishwife.

LOTTE: [*In a voice of thunder*] *Lettice!*

[LETTICE *jumps, badly startled. She turns and sees the outraged and bandaged woman in the wrecked doorway.*]

LETTICE: Lotte!

LOTTE: [*To* BARDOLPH] Turn that off, please!

BARDOLPH: I'm sorry?

LOTTE: *Off!* . . . Your machine. If you please.

BARDOLPH: You are Miss Schoen, I take it.

LOTTE: [*Raging*] Turn that damn thing off!

[LOTTE *advances, glaring, into the room and turns it off.*]

Now: You will ignore every word this woman has spoken.

BARDOLPH: What?

LOTTE: Every word.

BARDOLPH: I'm afraid I can't do that. She is making a statement to me. I am her solicitor.

LOTTE: Rubbish! Miss Douffet is a compulsive storyteller. I am surprised you haven't gathered that by now.

LETTICE: [*Protesting*] Lotte!

BARDOLPH: Do you mean she is lying?

LOTTE: I mean she is a romancer. Her word may not be relied on.

LETTICE: That's not true! How can you say that? Every word of that is fact! Every single word!

BARDOLPH: If you will excuse me, madam, this meeting is solely between me and my client. Your presence is quite improper.

LOTTE: This woman has been dismissed repeatedly from jobs for fabrication. I can produce countless witnesses to prove it!

LETTICE: Lotte!

LOTTE: If you bring one word of this into court I will summon people who will bear this out absolutely! Members of the Preservation Trust! Elizabethan scholars! Store managers on Oxford Street! . . . I advise you to delete every word of that tape and find some better defense for this lady.

[*A pause. She produces her cologne and handkerchief and applies it grimly.*]

LETTICE: It's true, then.

LOTTE: What?

LETTICE: You accused me. You told the police I assaulted you . . . Answer, please.

LOTTE: I don't know.

LETTICE: What do you mean?

[LOTTE *does not reply.*]

What do you mean, you don't know? [*Urgently*] *Answer me!*

LOTTE: [*Uncomfortably*] They came to me in hospital. I was doped up from medicine. I had the most terrible pain in my head. You know what my headaches are like at the best of times—without this!

LETTICE: [*Desperate*] *What did you say to them?*

LOTTE: *I can't remember!* They were only there a moment. One of the officers said to me, "You've been hit by your friend with an axe: Is that right?" I suppose I said yes . . . Well, it was the truth.

LETTICE: But not attacked! You weren't *attacked!*

LOTTE: I didn't say I was.

LETTICE: They assumed you *did!* That's how it must have sounded!

LOTTE: [*Petulant*] I was weak! I was so weak, and my

head was splitting . . . I didn't realize what I was imply-
ing!

LETTICE: [*Crying out*] And for that I am being *tried!*
. . . I'm going to be tried—in *reality!* . . . In a *real court!*

[*A pause.*]

LOTTE: I know.

LETTICE: So then I must tell the truth. I have to explain.

LOTTE: No!

LETTICE: I have to tell them how it happened. To put
things right.

LOTTE: Not with that. [*Pointing at the tape machine*] You
can't use that. I forbid it.

LETTICE: Well, what am I to do? Go to prison?

LOTTE: That won't happen.

LETTICE: Of course it will. Attempted murder!

LOTTE: Nonsense.

LETTICE: That's the charge!

BARDOLPH: [*Tentatively*] Excuse me—

LOTTE: There's always a way. We'll think of something.

LETTICE: What way? I am charged, Lotte! What else can
I say?

LOTTE: *Invent* something, for heaven's sake! You've
never been slow at it before!

BARDOLPH: [*Bolder*] Excuse me—

LETTICE: [*Joyfully*] At least—at least you didn't betray
me! That's all that really matters.

LOTTE: What?

LETTICE: I thought the most dreadful things about you.
I'm sorry, but it looked so bad.

LOTTE: What do you mean?

LETTICE: I thought you'd denounced me. That you told
them I did it on purpose.

LOTTE: Why on earth should I say that?

BARDOLPH: [*Overbearing them*] *Excuse me!*

LOTTE: [*Turning on him sharply*] Yes!—What?

BARDOLPH: Am I to understand that in your view Miss Douffet is innocent of this charge?

LOTTE: Of course she is!

BARDOLPH: And everything I have heard so far on this tape about playing games of execution is in fact true?

[*A pause.*]

Please reply.

LOTTE: Yes . . . [*Pause.*] All the same, it must not be used.

BARDOLPH: I'm afraid it may have to be. If your wound was received in the course of one of these games, it would obviously be highly relevant.

LOTTE: Don't you utter another word, Lettice! Not one more syllable—do you understand me?

BARDOLPH: Miss Schoen, please—let me continue with my questions. Miss Douffet, you are in the middle of a statement to your legal representative. If you wish to avoid extremely unpleasant consequences, I suggest you continue with it *now* . . . [*Pleading*] I have to hear the end of your story before I can advise you what to do.

[*A longer pause.*]

LETTICE: Yes. I shall continue.

BARDOLPH: Most wise.

[*He presses the tape recorder button.*]

LETTICE: I'm sorry, Lotte.

BARDOLPH: You do not have to remain if you don't wish, Miss Schoen.

[LOTTE *ignores him and sits down firmly in the Fal-staff chair.*]

LETTICE: [*Desperately, to her*] What else can I *do?*

[LOTTE *ignores her, too, staring straight ahead.*]

BARDOLPH: One thing has been puzzling me since you began to speak. You say this lady has always played the role of executioner and you of victim.

LETTICE: Correct!

BARDOLPH: Then, in fact, it would surely be she who would be holding any axe—not you.

[*A pause.*]

LETTICE: We swapped.

BARDOLPH: I'm sorry?

LETTICE: We exchanged roles. It was a wonderful moment, if I may say so . . . Lotte—Miss Schoen—elected herself to play the victim. She suggested it, not I. She came over to me as usual—

BARDOLPH: This was the day of the accident?

LETTICE: Yes. January the thirtieth. The anniversary of the beheading of Charles I in 1649. Charles the Martyr. She said to me—and it must have cost her a great effort—"*I* want to play the King tonight! I'm tired of prosecutors and executioners!" I was so happy. It represented—so much! . . . [*To* LOTTE] I'm sorry, but it did. It was wonderful when you asked.

[LOTTE *turns her head away.*]

[*To* BARDOLPH] Of course I said, "Yes, yes—of course: *Do it!* It's perfect for you, that part!" And it was! It absolutely was! She was truly glorious in it! [*To him*] I'd always played the role before, but nowhere near so well as she did it that night! . . . Her dignity in the trial was perfection! "I deny your right," she said—just like that: so proud and clear. "I deny with all my breath and being your right to judge me! I will enter the shining portal of Heaven with only this on my lips." It was sublime.

LOTTE: [*Cold and removed*] I didn't actually say any of that.

LETTICE: You did.

LOTTE: Not remotely.

LETTICE: You did, Lotte. I can hear it now.

LOTTE: Rubbish! You're "improving"—as usual. There was no "breath and being" and no "portal of Heaven," shining or otherwise. That is typical *you.*

LETTICE: Well, what *did* you say?

LOTTE: I'm sure your lawyer does not need the exact wording. Continue if you must, and leave me out of it.

LETTICE: [*Stubbornly*] Not until I have heard what you actually said.

LOTTE: Oh, for God's sake! What *anyone* would say playing that part! What Charles actually did say, of course. [*Brisk*] "I would know by what authority I am brought here. The Commons of England was never a judicial court. I would first know when it came to be so." Plain and simple, and very intelligent. A rarity around here.

LETTICE: I sit corrected.

BARDOLPH: Please go on.

LETTICE: Well . . . she rose finally, and I must say I could not have imagined a better rise from a throne. She stood with all the passion of the Stuarts surging through her—passion such as we have never witnessed in any monarch since! Rise, Lotte—show him. I dare you to do it again!

[LOTTE *folds her arms intransigently.*]

You *are* difficult, really . . . The point was, in a masterly transition she actually *became* the king, walking to his martyrdom! I've never seen anything better done. First she asked for one of my blouses and put it over her own—to represent the two shirts he wore against the cold. A clever touch, don't you think?

BARDOLPH: [*Getting caught up*] Most imaginative, certainly.

LETTICE: And then she embarked on the last solemn journey across St. James's Park to the balcony at Whitehall—and made it *unforgettable!* She simply walked—[*Pause*] I don't know how she did it, but she simply walked around this room, her head erect, and I saw it all. The freezing sunless morning—the company of nervous infantry—the slim, bearded man all in black, walking steadfastly over the frosty grass toward his death. Muffled drums sounded all the way—that was my part, of course, the muffled drums—big ones and little ones both beating out the knell of the last true monarch. Pam-tititi-pam! . . . Pam-tititi-pam! . . . Pam-tititi-pam! . . . Pam-tititi-pam! . . . [*To* LOTTE] Won't you help me? Show him what you did?

[LOTTE *turns grimly away from her.*]

All right, I'll do it alone. It won't be as good, but I'll show him.

LOTTE: [*Low*] Don't be stupid.

LETTICE: I will! [*Miming the drums*] Pam-tititi-pam!
. . . Pam-tititi-pam!

LOTTE: [*Through gritted teeth*] Lettice—stop it now!

[LETTICE *starts to march around the room, playing her invisible drum.*]

LETTICE: Pam-tititi-pam! . . . Pam-tititi-pam! . . . All the drums of London beating out together! [*Louder*] *Pam-tititi-pam! Pam-tititi-pam! Pam-tititi-pam! Pam-tititi-pam!*

LOTTE: [*Exploding over this*] Lettice! Stop this at *once!* You are making a complete fool of yourself! This has nothing whatever to do with anything!

BARDOLPH: Excuse me, but I think it has, Miss Schoen. I would very much like to see what occurred next.

LETTICE: [*Defiantly*] And so you shall! We came to the execution block: That's what happened next. The bloodstained, wooden block of execution!

BARDOLPH: What did you actually use for that? That stool perhaps?

LETTICE: [*Loftily*] Certainly not. We're not amateurs. We can do better than that, I hope . . . Behold! *Voilà!*

[*She whisks the black shawl off the big shape to reveal an executioner's block.*]

BARDOLPH: [*Impressed*] Where on earth did you find that?

LETTICE: [*Secretively*] Ah-ha!

BARDOLPH: It's not real? It can't possibly be real! . . . Is it?

LETTICE: What do *you* think?

BARDOLPH: I don't know . . . Tell me.

LETTICE: Guess. What would you say?

[*A pause. He examines it.*]

BARDOLPH: I'm not sure . . . I can't tell . . . Yes!

[LETTICE *laughs delightedly.*]

LETTICE: Ah-ha! Fooled you!

BARDOLPH: It *isn't?*

LETTICE: No! But it looks perfect, doesn't it? Isn't it absolutely perfect?

BARDOLPH: I'd never have known!

LETTICE: No one would! We looked for a real one, of
course. [*To* LOTTE] We actually looked for ages, didn't
we? We searched all the antique shops in London, just
about. The Portobello Road—Islington Market . . . I
scoured the catalogs of Sotheby's and Christie's. There
wasn't one to be found. Don't you think that's odd?

BARDOLPH: Well, yes—now you come to mention it. I
mean, there must have been blocks all over England at
one time.

LETTICE: Exactly. As you can imagine we were in despair,
because we needed one desperately. Until she had her
inspiration. Tell him, Lotte.

[*Pause.*]

BARDOLPH: [*To* LOTTE] Please . . . I'm most interested.
How did you solve the problem?

LOTTE: [*Grimly*] I used my brains. If one wishes to find
a block, where does one go?

BARDOLPH: I really can't think: Where?

LOTTE: To a forest, naturally.

BARDOLPH: So where did you go?

LETTICE: Epping. It's only about twenty miles. She was

quite right—there were hundreds of suitable logs strewn about. It was just a question of shaping one.

BARDOLPH: [*Now deeply involved*] But how did you get it home? By taxi?

LOTTE: Of course not. Do you imagine we can afford taxis from Epping Forest to Earl's Court? We took a bus. The driver was most uncooperative.

LETTICE: He said he wasn't paid to carry lumber.

LOTTE: Pedantic man.

LETTICE: But she was brilliant! She said, "We are fungus experts from the Ministry of Health. We have found a very rare variety of fungus growing on this log. It could prove of the utmost benefit to medical research, provided it is not disturbed."

BARDOLPH: Most inspired.

LOTTE: [*Coldly*] Thank you.

BARDOLPH: So now we come to the execution. I presume that is where the accident occurred.

LETTICE: Oh, yes; I'm afraid so.

BARDOLPH: Please show me in detail, if you can.

LETTICE: That's easy. Lotte, you've got to do this. It's evidence.

LOTTE: Just describe it, Lettice. It doesn't need illustration.

BARDOLPH: I would rather it had it, if you don't mind. I would like an absolutely clear picture for counsel. We can do without the axe, of course.

LOTTE: You'll have to. The police removed it.

LETTICE: [*Seizing the property sword from the wall*] Never mind—I'll use this instead! It's a bit blunt but you can imagine it sharp . . . Lotte? Please! . . . It'll help me very much . . . *Please!* . . .

[*Glaring,* LOTTE *shrugs and rises under protest.*]

LOTTE: Go on, then.

LETTICE: She came forward onto the balcony where all was made ready—the whole scene draped in black. First she "with her keener eye the axe's edge did try": that's Andrew Marvell—a true poet. Then she knelt down and looked up at me playing her hapless executioner—kneel, Lotte, please.

[LOTTE *kneels, tight-lipped.*]

Now speak your line. *Lotte!*

LOTTE: [*Swiftly*] Do not strike until I extend my hand so.

LETTICE: [*West Country accent*] Nay, I will not, an't please Your Majesty.

LOTTE: [*As before*] Good fellow. I thank you.

[*She stretches herself over the block.*]

LETTICE: And then suddenly—suddenly I realized there was something wrong! . . . Do you know the most extraordinary fact about King Charles's death? The executioner was so frightened of being identified by the mob—the man who actually struck the head off his monarch's shoulders—both he and his assistant appeared in total disguise. Not just in a mask—*a false beard and false hair.* Truly. [*To* LOTTE] I'm right, aren't I?

LOTTE: So I understand.

LETTICE: Indeed some people said it was actually *Oliver Cromwell himself* disguised like that. I myself hardly dare believe it—*but what a story if it were true!* . . . Well, anyway, I had totally forgotten to put them on. Can you believe such stupidity?—and it's the best thing about my whole part, the disguise. So I simply halted proceedings. Keeping dead in character, I said: [*West Country accent, confidential*] "Excuse me, Your Majesty. I foind I am without my foinal trappings. Pray give me leave to go and fetch 'em." She nodded curtly, brilliantly taking up the cue—She nodded curtly, Lotte—[LOTTE *nods curtly.*]—and I retreated to the bedroom to put them on. Like this.

[*She retreats backward to the bedroom, bowing to her king all the way. She opens the bedroom door.* LOTTE *sits up in alarm.*]

LOTTE: *No! No!* Stop it now!

LETTICE: I can't! This is the best bit!

LOTTE: [*Panic in her voice*] Is she still there? Is she still in there?

LETTICE: Of course not! How could she be? . . . [*Irate*] Who did you think was going to look after her while I was in custody—*you?* . . . She was given away, the poor thing.

BARDOLPH: What are you talking about now? . . . You were getting your disguise.

LETTICE: I still am. And you are going to help me.

BARDOLPH: I?!

LETTICE: You're going to be the drums. I had to do them myself last time and it didn't work at all. Now you can fill in while I dress.

BARDOLPH: I couldn't.

LETTICE: Of course you can. It's just a sound.

BARDOLPH: No, I really couldn't!

LETTICE: You *must,* or we'll lose all the tension! Imagine them—beating all down Whitehall, hundreds of drums, without remorse of voice! . . . Pam-tititi-pam! . . . Pam-

tititi-pam! . . . [*Pleading*] Try it, Mr. Bardolph. It can
really be thrilling if you do it properly . . . Won't you—
please? . . . [*Showing him, with solemn hand gestures*]
Pam-tititi-pam! . . . Pam-tititi-pam!

BARDOLPH: [*Imitating reluctantly and off the beat*] Pam-
tititi-pam . . . Pam-tititi-pam . . .

[LETTICE *shakes her head.*]

LETTICE: More menace. It has to have more menace . . .
Remember these were the most dreadful drums in England. They were announcing the end of everything.

BARDOLPH: What do you mean?

LETTICE: All the color! The age of color! The painted
churches! The painted statues! The painted language!
They're all about to go forever—at one stroke of an axe!
In their place will come gray! The great English gray!
The gray of Cromwell's clothes! The gray of Prose and
Puritanism, falling on us like a blight forever! [*Pause.*]
Play your role, Mr. Bardolph! It is a great one! The
honest yeoman wearing the helmet and breastplate
against his will—beating out on his drum the end of old
England! . . . Let them hear it now! Fill the snowy
streets of London with it! [*Louder*] *Pam-tititi-pam!*
. . . *Pam-tititi-pam!* . . . Come on now, Mr. Bardolph—
steady and terrible! *Pam-tititi-pam! . . . Pam-tititi-pam!*

[*Seduced,* BARDOLPH *joins in.*]

BARDOLPH: Pam-tititi-pam! Pam-tititi-pam!

LETTICE: That's *it! Excellent!* . . . Steady and terrible
that's the secret . . . steady and terrible!

BARDOLPH: [*Growing more and more committed*] Pam-
tititi-pam! . . . Pam-tititi-pam!

LETTICE: *Bravo!*

[*Suddenly he begins to march around the room to his own beat.* LOTTE, *on her knees, stares at him dumbfounded.*]

[*Clapping; delighted*] *Bravo,* Mr. Bardolph! Well done... Keep it up! . . . *Let all England hear you!*

[*She watches for a second—then slips into the bedroom as the lawyer, transported, moves uninhibitedly around the room at a slow and menacing march, banging his invisible drum and calling out his* pam-tititi-pams *with increasing excitement.* LOTTE *watches in amazement. Suddenly from the bedroom we hear* LETTICE'*s voice join his in wild soprano doubling. Their noise rises in a crescendo.*]

BARDOLPH and LETTICE: Pam-tititi-pam! . . . Pam-tititi-pam! . . . Pam-tititi-pam! . . . Pam-tititi-pam!!!

[*Abruptly the duet breaks off.* LETTICE *has reappeared. She stands before the astonished lawyer in her disguise, holding the sword at attention with both hands. She wears her black Mary Queen of Scots cloak, only back to front; over her eyes is a black executioner's mask; over her chin is a false ginger beard; over her head, completing an appearance of the utmost grotesqueness, is* LOTTE'*s discarded and of course ill-fitting wig.* BARDOLPH *stares at her, open-mouthed.* LOTTE *turns away, refusing to look. A pause.*]

LETTICE: Never forget—the most brilliant period in English history was brought to an end by a man looking like this. [*She advances into the room.*] The rest is quick to tell. I raised the axe—[*Demonstrating with the sword*]

and *she* came in! . . . I'd forgotten, you see, to close this
door.

BARDOLPH: [*Bewildered*] Who? . . . Who came in?

LETTICE: Felina, Queen of Sorrows.

BARDOLPH: *Who?*

LETTICE: My cat. Lotte is terrified of cats. And of course
Felina, the wicked thing, knew it. She bounded in—saw
Lotte there on the floor—and simply jumped with all
claws—right on top of her. Like this—*MEOW!*

> [LETTICE *jumps on* LOTTE *with claws extended.*
> LOTTE *jumps up in shock.*]

LOTTE: *Get off!* . . .

> [LETTICE *drops the sword.*]

LETTICE: Poor Lotte jerked right up in the air! I was so
startled I dropped the axe right on her. Just like that! It
was dreadful! . . . Oh, it was so dreadful! . . . There was
blood everywhere! She was moaning and crying, and
suddenly there was this banging on the door . . . I
couldn't get up and answer it—she was in such a state!
I was trying to quiet her—and then the door just burst
open and fell in. Exactly as you see it now.

BARDOLPH: And there was a policeman.

LETTICE: Yes . . . The rest you know.

> [*A long pause.* MR. BARDOLPH *wipes his brow with
> his handkerchief.*]

BARDOLPH: Well . . . [*To* LOTTE] There's only one thing
you can do, I'm afraid. You'll have to turn hostile.

LOTTE: I beg your pardon?

BARDOLPH: It's a phrase. Since you are the prosecution

witness you'll have to go into the box. Miss Douffet's barrister will cross-examine you. On your oath you must tell him precisely what I've just heard. That's what's called "turning hostile witness." The prosecution will of course ask the judge to take appropriate action.

LOTTE: Which is what?

BARDOLPH: To release Miss Douffet. There's obviously no case to answer.

[*He puts away the tape recorder in his briefcase.*]

LOTTE: And that's all?

BARDOLPH: He may permit himself a few pleasantries at your expense . . . An Englishwoman's home is her scaffold—and so forth. You know judges . . . If it's Justice Gasgoine, which I think it may well be, things could be a little rougher.

LOTTE: What do you mean?

BARDOLPH: He'll almost certainly give you a lecture about wasting the time of the court. [*Very dry voice*] "I find it extraordinary that two ladies of mature years have nothing better to do than behave like a couple of feeble-witted schoolgirls." That kind of thing.

LOTTE: Yes. I see. Thank you.

[*She looks grimly at* LETTICE, *who flinches.*]

Are you done here now?

BARDOLPH: I think so. Telephone me in the morning, Miss Douffet, if you would. I cannot, of course, call you.

LETTICE: [*Looking at* LOTTE; *subdued*] Yes.

BARDOLPH: Well, good-bye. I'll have all this written up and sent around to your counsel. With a note, of course.

LETTICE: Yes.

[*He goes to the stairs.*]

BARDOLPH: At least you won't have to go to prison. That's
comforting, isn't it? A little embarrassment and it's all
over.

LETTICE: All over, yes . . .

LOTTE: [*Cold*] Good-bye, Mr. Bardolph.

BARDOLPH: Good-bye . . . Good-bye, Miss Douffet . . .

[*He extends his hand. She takes it. He tries to convey
his sense of pleasure in having encountered her.*]

I—I—I really . . . [*But cannot.*] Good-bye.

[*He goes, hastily, taking his briefcase. We see his legs
disappear upstairs. A pause. The two ladies stand, not
looking at each other. The front door slams.* MR. BAR-
DOLPH's *legs come down the front steps above and
walk past the house out of sight.*]

LETTICE: You're very angry, aren't you?

LOTTE: [*Very cold*] Why should I be angry? A woman
whose life has just been ruined.

LETTICE: [*Timid*] That's not absolutely true.

LOTTE: Not? How else would you put it?

LETTICE: All he said was "a little embarrassment." That's
not ruin.

LOTTE: I was promoted last week. I am now head of the
department.

LETTICE: [*Pleased*] Oh!

LOTTE: When this comes out I shall be its laughing-stock.
In fact, the laughing-stock of London, when they read
their papers . . . We both will be: But in your case it
scarcely matters, does it?

LETTICE: [*Shocked*] Lotte!

LOTTE: I am a respected woman in a responsible and enviable job. After the trial I'll never be able to enter my office again . . . I will resign first thing in the morning.

LETTICE: No!

LOTTE: What else would you advise? Stay on and ignore the giggles? Pretend not to hear the whispers? You've done for me, Lettice. It's only just: I recognize that. Tit for tat. Perfect justice.

LETTICE: What are you talking about?

LOTTE: I dismiss you. You dismiss me. Revenge is sweet.

LETTICE: That's not fair!

LOTTE: It's absolutely right!

LETTICE: That's not fair at all!

LOTTE: *Fair?!* I join you, my dear, in the ranks of the Unemployed! Where I believe fairness is not the salient characteristic! Or I could sell tea towels in one of our remoter gift shops.

[*She gives* LETTICE *a ghastly smile. A bitter pause.*]

Actually I deserve it. I deserve it all. I let you do it.

LETTICE: Do what?

LOTTE: Lure me.

LETTICE: Lure?

LOTTE: Into your world. An actress's world. [*Harshly*] No—*not even an actress!* . . . Here.

[*She takes the keys of the flat out of her bag and drops them on the Falstaff chair.*]

LETTICE: You must know I am guiltless. Unwittingly I have brought embarrassment on you. That seems to be my allotted role—but it is not my purpose. Revile me if you wish. Spurn me, I don't blame you. Only know—I

would truly sooner cut this hand off than injure one
hair—one single hair in that corolla of gray!

LOTTE: Oh, stop it! STOP IT! Listen to yourself! "Guiltless" . . . "Spurn" . . . "Revile" . . . "Corolla"! . . . *Who
are you being now?*

[*A pause.* LETTICE *looks at her, bewildered.*]

LETTICE: [*Simply*] Myself . . . Myself.

[*A pause.*]

LOTTE: [*Factual*] Let's not go on. It's entirely my fault. If
one embraces the ridiculous, one ends up becoming
ridiculous.

LETTICE: [*Stricken*] Don't!

LOTTE: That's all there is to it. Good-bye.

[*She goes up the stairs.*]

LETTICE: No!

[*She runs after her and calls up desperately from the
bottom stair.*]

No. *You wanted it.* You said so often. "That awful
desk—the *Non-doer's Desk*. If only I could leave it and
never see it again!"

[LOTTE *pauses.*]

You said that over and over!

LOTTE: [*Hard*] So you decided to give me a push, is that
it? *Thank you!*

[*She goes on upstairs and out of the flat.*]

LETTICE: *Lotte!*

[*The front door slams.* LETTICE *looks about in panic, then dashes to the intercom telephone, and picks it up. We see* LOTTE's *legs starting to walk across the window.*]

[*Into the phone*] *Wait!!* . . . [*The legs halt.*] That's stupid—just *going!* We can think of *something* for you! There's always something! Even for *me*—there's *something!*

[*A pause.*]

[*In a voice of sudden defeat*] No. Actually, no . . . *Not* for me . . . [*Pause.*] You're wrong when you say there's nothing ghosty about me. That's what *I* am. A Ghost. Every day more. Every day there's something new I don't understand . . . It's like a mesh keeping me out— all the new things, *your* things. Computers. Screens. Bleeps and buttons. Processors. Every day more . . . Bank cards—phone cards—software—discs! JVC. PLC. ABC. DEF. [*More and more anguished*] The whole place—the whole world I understood isn't there . . . You talk about Europe gone—that's just buildings! *Everything*'s gone for me. I can't work any of it. *I'm* the foreigner—not Mr. Pachmani. It's all like that writing on my walls—just squiggles and dots. [*Flatly*] You're right. That's the precise word for me—ridiculous. Ridiculous and useless. [*Pause.*] Useless stories. Useless glories. Ridiculous and useless. [*Pause.*] I'm sorry. I haven't got anything else.

[*Abruptly she hangs up the receiver and stands crying helplessly. Equally abruptly* LOTTE *returns to the front door and presses the buzzer aggressively.*

[LETTICE *ignores it—but* LOTTE *insists. Finally* LETTICE *picks up the phone.*]

What?

LOTTE: [*Over speaker; sharply*] Let me in!

LETTICE: No.

LOTTE: [*Over speaker*] Do you hear me? Let me in at once. *Open it, Lettice.* [*Shouting*] *Press the damn thing!*

[LETTICE *presses the button. The front door opens above and slams.* LOTTE *storms down the stairs in outrage. She turns on the light at the bottom, making* LETTICE *shrink in its glare.*] *How dare you?* That's disgusting. Sniveling, feeble, whining rubbish! That's not you! *I won't have it. I won't stand for it, do you hear?* . . . How *can* you? . . . You're *Lettice!*

[LETTICE *turns away, hiding her head from the onslaught.*]

All right, I hated the job. You're right: I admit it. I'm glad to be done with it—all right! That doesn't mean I'm going to spend the rest of my life hiding in the Past . . . Are you listening?

LETTICE: [*Not looking at her*] I don't hide.

LOTTE: Of course you do! You're like those women in my office! [*In a "refined" voice*] "Oh, dear! Oh, dear, dear, dear!—this horrid nasty *Present!*" . . . [*Hard*] The Past was just as nasty as we are! Just as stupid! Just as greedy and brutal!

LETTICE: No!

LOTTE: *Worse!* For most people it was far worse! Superstitious and sordid and violent! Far more painful and far more unjust!

LETTICE: [*Hotly*] At least it had beauty! You said that yourself! "It gets uglier every minute!" you said.

LOTTE: So it does!

LETTICE: So why shouldn't I hide? It's hideous here! Everywhere! . . . *Hideous and hateful!*

LOTTE: Then do something about it! *Fight it! Attack it!* Show some *spunk,* for God's sake! Don't just stay cringing in a basement, playing stupid games!

LETTICE: [*Desperate*] Well, what can I *do?!* . . . What can *you* do?—or *anyone?* . . . *Look* at us!

LOTTE: I *am* looking. . . . We are two able, intelligent women. *I* am an experienced organizer of tours. *You* are without a doubt the most . . . original tour guide. That must give us something.

LETTICE: What?

LOTTE: We're a combination. We could work together.

LETTICE: [*Bewildered*] What do you mean? How? . . . *How?* . . .

LOTTE: [*Suddenly excited*] I have it! . . . I really do! . . . Look—do you remember the organisation I proposed— the E.N.D.? The Eyesore Negation Detachment? Well, what if we *revived* it?—in another form! Not bombs— Tours! Why don't we start our own firm—*E.N.D. Tours*—dedicated to showing tourists *the fifty ugliest new buildings in London!*—How about *that?* I can provide the architectural information—You can speak it: in your own inimitable way! You lit up the Past with a blazing torch, people said—well now light up in the Present! Reveal the ugliness for what it is!

LETTICE: Oh, Lotte!

LOTTE: I could advertise everywhere! Send leaflets into every travel agency in Britain—even America, why not? Even Americans must get fed up with history *sometimes*—and they certainly won't *ever* have seen anything like this! [*Theatrically*] "E.N.D. Tours presents Lettice Douffet's Dramatic Guide to Disgusting Buildings! Hear her Devastating Denunciations of Modern Design! Before your very eyes she will show you how Beauty has been murdered—and by whom! Exactly which Architects, Builders, Engineers, and City Planners! See her point the finger! Hear her name the names!"

LETTICE: Oh, that's marvelous!

LOTTE: It could work! . . . Ten pounds for each excursion!

LETTICE: [*Transported*] It's tremendous! It's the single most theatrical idea I ever heard! [*Ardently*] *Oh, my mother would have been so proud of you!* [*Pause.*] Let's imagine it—how it could go! . . . We are in some vast, horrible office building, surrounded by a huge group of tourists—hanging on my every word! . . . [*Interrupting herself*] Do you think I should have a uniform?

LOTTE: Oh, definitely!

LETTICE: Something crisp and authoritarian.

LOTTE: And a cap with E.N.D. written around the brim in gold thread!

LETTICE: Perfect! . . . I can see it now! . . . [*Speaking ringingly to her imaginary audience*] Ladies and Gentlemen—You are standing in the main entrance hall of . . . [*Inventing*] Computex House.

LOTTE: Oh splendid! "Computex!"

LETTICE: "Constructed in 1980 out of British concrete. Observe the cracks, splits, and damp-stains, typical of the period! [LOTTE *laughs*] The obvious intention of this award-winning building is to resemble as much as possible a Top-security prison! Please note the thousand metal-framed windows—not one of which can be opened."

LOTTE: And made out of tinted solar glass—that's its name—to insure a perpetually gloomy interior!

LETTICE: "Substituting for the ghastly glare of sunshine the glorious glow of fluorescence."

LOTTE: Excellent!

[LETTICE *moves to the staircase and takes her position exactly as in Act one, Scene one.*]

"Over here we find the Central Staircase, consisting of seven hundred depressing steps in artificial stone."

LOTTE: "Granolithic compound," please.

LETTICE: "Note how its tiers of tubular steel struts cleverly emphasize the motif of Incarceration."

[LOTTE *laughs again.* LETTICE *addresses the audience out front a little more directly.*]

"Ladies and Gentlemen—these grim stairs were recently the scene of the most dramatic protest yet to be made in Britain by ordinary people against modern brutalist architecture. Last Christmas Eve, a brilliant snowy night—though nobody could see it because of the tinted solar glass—six typists, unable to bear the prospect of working in this place another day, walked up all seven hundred gray and granolithic steps—joined hands on the topmost landing up there [*She points upward*] can you see it?—and together hurled themselves into the stairwell below, singing the Hallelujah Chorus. They landed *precisely where I stand now!* . . . For this reason it is now known as the Staircase of Secretarial Solace."

LOTTE: [*Laughing*] You are incorrigible! You really are!

LETTICE: And you're dazzling, Lotte! It's a dazzling idea! *We'll make a fortune!*

LOTTE: But wait!—I have a perfect thought for the end! When you finish—just before you dismiss them—we give them all a present. Something they won't be expecting at all.

LETTICE: What?

[*Delightedly* LOTTE *fetches from the back of the room a tray bearing the two jeweled goblets and the gilded bottle of quaff.*]

LOTTE: Ladies and Gentlemen, E.N.D. Tours takes pride in offering you—after the aesthetic horrors you have endured—a complimentary beverage. Please drink deep. This cordial is not meant to trickle down the throat but to cascade.

LETTICE: *Bravo!*

LOTTE: And then I'll say—[*Pouring the liquor*] "It is entirely the inspiration of my colleague, Miss Lettice Douffet—a lady of countless inspirations. It offers in miniature what she herself offers in bounteous measure. Enlargement for shrunken souls—Enlivenment for dying spirits—Enlightenment for dim, prosaic eyes. In short—Lovage."

[*Music sounds, antique and tender.* LOTTE *offers* LETTICE *one goblet and takes the other herself.*]

LETTICE: [*To the audience*] This concludes our tour for today. On behalf of Miss Schoen and myself—a *brimming* good-bye to you!

[*The two ladies swirl their goblets in unison.*]

BOTH: One—two—three—*Quaff!*

[*They raise their goblets with both hands, toasting the audience as the music swells and the curtain falls.*]

END OF PLAY

ABOUT THE AUTHOR

Peter Shaffer was born in Liverpool, England, in 1926. During the Second World War he worked as a conscript in a coal mine; later he studied history on a scholarship to Cambridge University, and departed thence to New York. There he worked in a Doubleday bookstore, and the Forty-second Street library, living for much of the time in Hell's Kitchen, and returning three years later to London, convinced of his own unemployability. In some desperation he wrote his first play, *Five Finger Exercise,* which was produced in 1958 to widespread approval (in New York in 1959, where it won the Drama Critics Award), thereby relieving him of the necessity of working in other stores or offices.

The success of his first play suggested to Shaffer that he might be a dramatist at heart. Partly because he felt he had no aptitude for doing anything else, he sat down during the ensuing years and produced other plays. All of these met with great success, first in London and then in New York: *The Private Ear* and *The Public Eye,* a double bill, in 1962; *The Royal Hunt of the Sun,* an epic concerning the conquest of Peru, which Bernard Levin described as "the greatest play of our generation," in 1964; and in the following year *Black Comedy,* a romp which another London critic hailed as "the farce of the century." In 1970 Peter Shaffer wrote *The Battle of Shrivings* (published in an altered form as *Shrivings*) and in 1973 *Equus,* which ran for over a thousand performances on Broadway, winning the Tony Award and the Drama Critics Award. *Amadeus* was the fourth successful play Shaffer originated at the National Theatre of Great Britain: it opened on Broadway in December 1980, where it too ran for over a thousand performances and also won the Tony Award. This was followed in 1985 by *Yonadab,* a complex drama involving the turbulent family of King David, and then *Lettice & Lovage.*

Peter Shaffer divides his time between New York City and London. In 1987 he was made a Commander of the Order of the British Empire.